There's something going on upstairs

There's Something Going On Upstairs

*Learning to Laugh My Way
through a Cancerous Brain Tumor,
One Chemo Cycle at a Time*

Kelly Fosso Rodenberg

Library of Congress Control Number: 2019913398

ISBN, print   978-0-578-56288-9
ISBN, ebook   978-0-578-56294-0

Manufactured in the United States of America

23   22   21   20   19   1   2   3   4   5   6   7   8   9   10

With Gratitude

To my dad in heaven.

*You taught me to have faith, count my blessings,
stay strong, pray each day, work hard, do chores,
and keep on the sunny side of life.*

I miss you every single day.

Contents

Author's Note   ix

Prologue   xi

1. Backspace Bonanza   1

2. This Is Your Time to Shine 7

3. Soil and Water   10

4. Jumping Ship   14

5. A Couple of Case Studies   20

6. Go Time   24

7. There's No Place Like Home   30

8. Head Hardware   33

9. Home for the (Early) Holidays   39

10. My Church Pew Analogy   43

11. Head-Shave Day   47

12. Attacking the Floor   49

13. Winter in Minnesota   51

14. Normal around Here
    Is Just a Setting on the Dryer   55

15. The Canary in the Corner 63

16. Choose to Live Life Anyway 66

17. The Room of Common Denominators 68

18. Fifty Shades of Gray 74

19. So What's Your Prognosis? 81

20. Taking It All in Stride 84

21. Precious, Precious Moments 86

22. Atta Girl, Alexa 89

23. Putting the Pieces Together 95

24. Platelet Mambo: How Low Can You Go? 97

25. Emotional Mess Express 99

26. We Are Stronger Together 101

27. The Here and Now 106

Epilogue 113

Author's Note

Hi, I'm Kelly Rodenberg. I am fiftyish and live in Chaska, Minnesota, now, but I grew up in a mystical, magical, fairy-tale place—a farm in Kandiyohi County. From as young as my mom would probably allow, I thrived on being outside, helping my dad and brother with chores. It rarely mattered what kind of chores; I just loved being outside helping, which probably explains my never-been-used KitchenAid mixer today.

Oh, don't worry, I started out with very small tasks: watering the hogs, scooping feed into pails, sweeping the shop floor, and sorting like-sized nuts, bolts, and washers into empty coffee cans. Eventually I moved up to running after and catching the newborn piglets so Dad could administer their vaccinations.

On those in-between days when I was too little to work on whatever project Dad was doing at the time, I'd impatiently ask, "Dad, what can I do to help?"

Like clockwork he'd reply, "Just stand there and look beautiful." Sweaty, snotty-nosed, and tangle-haired as I was, I did my best.

Next came filling silage wheelbarrows, feeding cows, and carrying those previously filled feed pails. It was probably my claim to fame—carrying four five-gallon feed pails at once, two with each hand—that earned me the nickname Horse.

On occasion my older brother, Lonnie, and I may or may not have been known to fight while cleaning the hog barn. I'm sure he wanted to scrape the aroma one way and I wanted to scrape it the other.

Catching us in the arguing act, Dad would come over and say in a stern voice, "If you kids can't get along out here, get in the house, and I'll do it myself."

Let me back up: that was my severely *diabetic* dad. Worst assignment ever? Getting sent inside. While we did as we were told and went inside to our rooms, it wasn't long before we were back outside with our crocodile tears, begging, "Dad, Dad, can we *please* come out and clean the barn?"

Spectacular reverse psychology. Dad 1, dueling duo 0.

By the time my younger brother, Ryan, was on the scene, I'd graduated to picking rocks, pulling weeds, and riding the straw- and hay-bale rack, where my special girly talent was stacking bales six high. Dad always did claim I knew what the working end of a pitchfork was.

To my heavenly dad, hardworking mom, and two heart-warming brothers, thank you for your farming passion that remains today. It is your moral fiber, resilience, and work ethic that built me into the fighter I am. Know that I wouldn't trade where I grew up, when I grew up, or how I grew up for the world.

Prologue

I give. About fifty people have encouraged me to write a book. No, I haven't literally been keeping track, but after dozens of nudges, I began paying attention. My initial response? To casually laugh it off and think, *Sure, in my spare time.*

Mr. Welch's 1985 creative writing class at Willmar High School was one of my favorites. Embarrassingly, I've always treasured his circled red A+ at the top of my final paper and the words "This is college material" scribbled beneath it.

In March 2012 my husband, Bob, experienced excessive foot pain that brought us to Methodist Hospital and eventually to the Mayo Clinic, where doctors diagnosed him with a rare blood disorder called POEMS syndrome. POEMS is a shirttail relative to cancer and ultimately required a stem cell transplant. It's not a road you see yourself traveling less than two years into your marriage. We packed our MDX with everything we'd need to stay in a rented Rochester townhouse for six weeks, as we couldn't be more than ten minutes away from the clinic in case something adverse happened. Immediately I signed up for CaringBridge, for it was by far the easiest way to keep family and friends updated on his condition. Anyone who wanted could opt in to notifications and receive the same message at the same time. Brilliant! Journaling was therapeutic for me during those six months of medical treatments; as the sole caregiver, I found it to be a remarkable emotional outlet as I sat at my laptop after a long day at the clinic and wept. Bob beat the odds, and he has been in remission for nearly seven years. Hallelujah!

Fast-forward to 2018, and the shoe has switched to the other foot: I'm now the patient instead of the caregiver. In October I was diagnosed with an aggressive Glioblastoma–Grade 4 brain tumor between my frontal and parietal lobes.

Watching our struggle to keep loved ones updated, my sweet sister-in-law Sarah Fosso asked if she could set up a Caring-Bridge site on my behalf. What a godsend! Sarah is a busy farm-wife and mother of three very active kids: Emma, Elsa, and Harris. It wasn't as if she was sitting around with her feet up eating bonbons. Knowing this, I still took her up on her offer.

Sarah is also the one who realized Bob's diagnosis presented itself at the same time mine did—at fifty-two years of age. Immediately we determined that 5 + 2 could only mean one thing: lucky #7!

As I started feeling better, I was able to begin authoring a few CaringBridge updates on my own. Instantly, I recalled the comfort generated through writing. It was equally relaxing and healing to jot things down, especially when this particular curveball seemed so out of control.

A heartfelt thanks to all those who have encouraged these words. You gave me purpose—a reason to get up—in my darkest of days.

I've realized the final stage of healing is using what has happened to you to help others. If these words are able to help even one person walking a similar path, this book will be a win.

There's something going on upstairs

Backspace Bonanza

October 5, 2018

Something is off. Not noticeably or visibly off, I reason, but certainly off. As I work on my computer, handling normal admin projects, my emails begin to look strange—or shall I say stranger than normal. My replies take on a life of their own: "Ssssssure I can book the board rrrrroom for you." "Wwwwwhat time wwwwwould you like lunch?"

While I'm far from the perfect typist, these typos become majorly annoying. Backspace, backspace, backspace. I flex the fingers on my left hand.

Well, that's different, I muse. Feeling odd, I make a mental note.

Just over a week before this, I had enjoyed a wonderful massage identical to those I'd received nearly a hundred times before. I had asked the massage therapist to work on my neck and shoulders. Thirty years of computer work does have its hazards, after all. I left her office feeling refreshed as usual, but for the first time ever, my therapist suggested I go home and ice my shoulders a bit. Perhaps it wasn't an unusual request given the concentrated deep-tissue therapy, but for me it was a first. Upon arriving home, I broke out the ice pack for a few minutes. Still feeling refreshed, I slipped into bed all relaxed and confident I'd wake the next morning recharged for the next busy workday.

I awoke at 2:00 a.m. to what I can only explain as lightning bolts moving through my left wrist and fingers. Oddest feeling ever. As I turned on the dim overhead light, I actually saw my fingers involuntarily moving. My initial thought was that my delightful massage had resulted in a pinched nerve or something. It took some time, but eventually I drifted back into a sound sleep.

The next morning I told my husband, Bob, what had happened. It was, after all, a bizarre sensation I'd never felt before. Getting ready for work, I had trouble finding the left sleeve of my shirt and couldn't maneuver the clasp on my necklace. I certainly had been able to dress myself the previous morning, but for some reason, on this morning I needed help. I muddled through the next couple of days needing more and more help.

During that weekend, we had invited good friends Steve, Michele, Keith, Merrie, Doug, Lisa, Kevin, and Kyle over for a fall barbecue, a fun little get-together before heading into our long Minnesota winter. While I went about some inside hosting duties, Bob ran a few errands. Ever the thoughtful one, he came home with a carpal tunnel brace and asked me to wear it around the house, hoping it might help my hand. I hadn't experienced any more hand spasms, but while setting the kitchen island for our friends, I did notice my right hand was doing most of the heavy lifting. I could lift ten glass dinner plates out of the cupboard, but I had to tilt the majority of the weight onto my right hand. Why were these normal household tasks suddenly more challenging?

We laughed it up inside, then moved to the backyard for a few s'mores. Here I struggled with opening the graham cracker package and the chocolate bars. Hmmm, that was odd. Other things I added to the mental list. Difficult as it was, I tried to put on a cheery hosting face that evening; however, I didn't completely get away with it. A couple of weeks later, Michele said she could sense something was off.

"You just didn't seem like yourself," she confessed.

Putting all the mental notes from the past week or so aside,

I return to work, where I'm typing again: "I'm haaaaappy to rrrrreserve the cccccompany vehicle for you. Howwwww many days will you neeeeed it?"

More backspacing. Seriously? What is going on? In a one-on-one with my manager, I sense my left hand beginning to twitch. Not only is the sensation unusual, but I feel the immediate need to grasp it, just praying it goes unnoticed.

Following our meeting, I make my way to the kitchen for my weekday yogurt and apple. Not one to bite into fruit, I pull out the kitchenette drawer for a knife and begin slicing my apple into thin slices. Suddenly I notice blood on the countertop and wonder where in the world that came from. Looking down at my left hand, I see I've sliced the top of my thumb without feeling a thing. Absolutely, positively nothing about this seems normal.

Heading back to my desk, I make the executive decision to place a call to Park Nicollet. I give the appointment scheduler a rundown of my symptoms over the past ten days. Ten days? Has it seriously been only ten days? Double-checking the date of my massage, yes, it has been ten short days. I explain I had gotten a massage, was woken up by an electrical bolt running through my fingers, had trouble finding a left sleeve, made annoying typing mistakes at the office, needed help with sealed packages, cut my thumb, and overall was experiencing a lazy left hand.

"Let me take a look at our schedule," she replies. "The next available opening we have is two weeks from today."

Seriously, two weeks? While not at all comfortable with the wait, I have zero options and ask her to put me on the schedule.

"If you have a cancellation, could you please let me know?" I desperately ask before hanging up.

A few hours later I receive a call from a different Park Nicollet nurse. *Ah, an opening*, I hope.

She explains she had reviewed the phone transcripts from earlier in the day. She strongly suggests I go to a TRIA Orthopaedic Center for a walk-in appointment. "They could quickly tell you if it indeed is a pinched nerve," she encourages me.

A few days from now, I'll think of this unknown angel on the other end of the line as my Miracle #1. I discuss the calls and conversations with Bob over the weekend and decide to get myself in to TRIA.

October 9, 2018

When the receptionist at the Bloomington TRIA Orthopaedic Center requests my insurance card, I'm embarrassed when I'm unable to remove it from my wallet with my left hand.

"Can I help you?" the receptionist kindly asks.

"Yes, please. It's a new wallet," I falsely reply.

I complete their paperwork, and a nurse takes me to an exam room within a few minutes. Dr. Bugbee asks me to do some fundamental movements: touch my nose, walk a straight line, puff out my cheeks, and resist the pushing of his hands. After I pass his battery of tests with flying colors, he agrees it quite possibly could be a pinched nerve.

"We have a whole bundle of nerves right here," Dr. Bugbee says, pointing between his left shoulder and neck, "that run all the way down our arm, wrist, and hand. I could suggest you try a few different things, beginning with physical therapy. *Or* what I'd rather have you do is go see a neurologist."

Wait, what? Why on earth would he suggest a neurologist? I wonder.

With a stiff upper lip, I leave TRIA. Once I'm in my car in the parking garage, I call Bob in tears. Unbeknownst to me, the alternate recommendation from that white-coated man at TRIA is my Miracle #2.

Arriving home, I feel like a cat on a hot tin roof. Knowing I can't put this off, I power on my laptop and begin searching. The neurologist I connect with later that afternoon is also part of the Park Nicollet Clinic system and is located in the St. Louis Park Meadowbrook Building. Great, I know just where to go.

He has an opening late Friday afternoon. Realistically it's only three days away, but after the news I just received at TRIA, Friday seems like a lifetime from now. Then I realize the timing would work out well for Bob to join me, as he has Friday afternoons off. "I'll take it," I answer.

Assuming Friday's neurologist will ask for a rundown of events, I draft a Word document of my past ten days of symptoms. Perhaps this is for my own peace of mind too; considering how quickly this all developed, I don't want to overlook anything important. Sitting at my laptop reviewing the bullets in black and white, the list disturbs even me.

- Have problems typing with my left hand
- Can't open a Band-Aid, double-zipped ziplock bags, or most sealed packages
- Can't use fingernail clippers on my right hand
- Find it cumbersome to shut the car door and clasp my seat belt while in the driver's seat
- Feel involuntary twitching in my left hand
- Have trouble switching the inside front door lock of our home
- Can't hold a newspaper upright or turn pages of a magazine with my left hand
- Can't put in my contacts
- Need help buttoning tops, unhooking my bra, putting on zippered or buttoned pants, tying a shoe
- Feel that virtually every cover is childproof

- Drop absolutely everything with my left hand—including my iPhone and iPad Mini
- Struggle to grasp a plastic cup or keep a paper plate level with my left hand

Okay, to most of you the last item may not seem like life or death, but to those of us who prefer dining on fine Chinet and drinking from Solo cups, it potentially is a game changer.

I quickly begin to realize that my husband is far more patient with me than I am with me. I need to have compassion for myself, but it's hard. When folding a load of clothes from the dryer should take a quick ten minutes, with only one cooperating hand, it now takes close to thirty.

As I groan in anguish over the routine daily things that suddenly are a challenge, Bob patiently says, "Sweetie, let me help you."

Bob helps me get dressed, volunteers to cut my food (yes, even in public), clips the nails on my right hand, and even *shaves my right armpit*. If this isn't love, I don't know what is.

Unbeknownst to me, while we wait for the neurologist appointment, Bob places a Hail Mary call to Dr. Angela Dispenzieri at the Mayo Clinic in Rochester. Dr. D (as we call her) was his saving grace in 2012 when he was diagnosed with POEMS syndrome. Yes, she specializes in hematology rather than neurology, but she is a starting point, a straw we can grasp on to.

"This has nothing to do with me, but my wife," Bob explains to Dr. D's message-taking nurse.

The return call from Dr. D will quickly turn into Miracle #3.

This Is Your Time to Shine

2

October 12, 2018

Apprehensively, we drive to Methodist's Meadowbrook Building to meet with the neurologist. While we're typically never at a loss for words, this drive is different. You can literally hear a pin drop. Standing in line to check in, I notice the scar above the right ear of the gentleman standing in front of me. Little did I know I'd have a similar scar in just eighteen days.

Appreciatively, Dr. John Worley is a jovial doctor. He enters the room and breaks through the heavy atmosphere for both Bob and me. I'm sure he knows no one actually wants to find themselves in the office of a neurologist, so what a blessing it is to be greeted by his cheery personality.

I hand him my typed document of symptoms, which he instantly commends me for compiling. "This is very valuable," he says. "Can I make a copy of it?"

After another battery of simplistic tests—"Open your mouth, grasp my hand, kick your legs, flex your fingers, puff out your cheeks"—he then scoots his swivel chair directly in front of me and asks me to smile real big. Motioning for Bob to come over, he inquires if Bob had noticed the slight drop on the left side of my lip.

"No, that's different," Bob replies.

Instantly, my inner voice suggests that I probably haven't been smiling around my husband enough lately.

"Have you been going to work?" Dr. Worley asks.

"Sure, I drove there this morning," I reply.

"And you've had no headaches or balance issues?" he asks.

"No, just a troublesome left hand," I respond.

"Why don't you step outside and walk down the hall for me as straight as you can, as fast as you can. This is your time to shine," he jokes.

Sensing the heat is on, I set out to show him just exactly how smooth my stride is.

Shortly after I take off, I hear him whisper to Bob to step out into the hall. "See that?" the doctor quietly asks him.

Then in his normal voice, "Okay, Kelly, now turn around and come back."

What I presumed would be a straight A test suddenly feels like an epic fail. Back in our room, Dr. Worley explains I was slightly weaving as I walked down the clinic hall.

Settling into my chair and slipping my shoes back on, I can tell Dr. Worley is attempting to frame his words.

"I think there's something going on upstairs," he carefully explains. "I don't think it's here," he says, laying his hand on the front of his forehead, "but I think there possibly could be a tumor here," he continues, placing his hand over the center top of his head. "I'd like to get you in for an MRI yet tonight."

And just like that, the rug is pulled out from under our feet. This is way more serious than a pinched nerve or lazy left hand.

Dr. Worley's nurse informs us that Park Nicollet in Maple Grove has an MRI opening at 6:00 p.m. Hoping to get to the bottom of things, we set the appointment, then realize we need to obtain preauthorization from my Blue Cross Blue Shield insurance company.

Our ever-so-kind nurse spends more than two hours on hold with BCBS. Checking in with us every thirty minutes or so, she apologizes profusely and explains that nothing ever seems to happen this late in the day on a Friday, but she is not giving up yet.

Finally, it reaches the point in time where we can't comfortably make the drive to Maple Grove in Friday traffic, even if we had the preapproval.

"I'm so sorry, but we're going to have to pick this up again first thing Monday morning," the nurse apologizes.

Great, a weekend of conclusion jumping, I selfishly think.

Dr. Worley touches base before we leave. "So sorry about the wait," he says, "but do me a favor: if you sense *any* type of change over the weekend, please go directly to the emergency room, and you'll be able to get an immediate MRI."

If the air was thick on the drive there, the drive home is exponentially strained. My thoughts are running a million miles an hour. We reach our driveway in silence, get ourselves inside, and attempt to absorb Dr. Worley's preliminary prediction.

It takes every ounce of courage I possess, but I know I have to call my mom, Helen Fosso. She was well aware of the time of our appointment that afternoon, and given the extended time duration, I know she's worried.

"Hi, Mom," I muster.

"Kelly, what's going on?" she asks, in a far-from-normal voice.

"They think it's a brain tumor," I sob, "but we can't get in for an MRI until Monday."

I've made a few tough phone calls in my day, but this is by far the toughest. The last thing I want to do is give my mom something—or someone—else to worry about. We tearfully say goodbye, and I promise to let her know when the MRI is scheduled. As I hang up the phone, I sense that life is about to be turned upside down.

3

Soil and Water

October 13, 2018

Prior to our flurry of medical appointments, we had planned a party for Saturday. We decide to keep cool and carry on, giving ourselves a reprieve from the worry. Bunco lover that I am, we are looking forward to hosting thirty-five of the most fun-loving, loud-laughing, Lord of Life Lutheran peeps one would ever hope to meet. We moved from the Dayton/Maple Grove area to Chaska two years prior, and we had been looking forward to catching up with our dear friends for weeks.

After getting a few things crossed off the Saturday list, I step into the shower. I fill my left palm with shampoo, but now I can't find the top of my head with that hand. Shortly after that, I experience some balance issues. Getting dressed, I notice it's hard to stand, and I find I need to use the handrail just to climb three short steps from the garage into the house. Things are changing for sure. We give in and set out for the emergency room as Dr. Worley had advised.

Just as we step out the door, Bob receives a return call from Dr. D in Rochester and quickly reviews my symptoms with her. Putting the phone on speaker, he explains the pinched nerve routine, the appointment with Dr. Worley, and the MRI delay.

We listen carefully as she reassuringly says, "Well, you're headed to the right place. Anytime there are extremity issues involved, we think of the brain. I'd like to send an email to a few of my colleagues and get their take."

We gratefully accept her offer and hang up.

Before we reach the hospital, the phone rings again. Within

minutes of hitting Send, Dr. D had offers from three doctors of neurology at the Mayo Clinic.

"Get things checked out in Minneapolis," Dr. D encourages us. "But if for any reason you aren't happy with what you hear, or you just want a second opinion, I have the names of three other specialists who would welcome seeing her." Reinsert Miracle #3 here.

We arrive at Methodist Hospital's emergency room, and I'm immediately wheeled in for an MRI. I'm beyond scared. The MRI machine is large and noisy, so I'm wearing earplugs and have pads on either side of my head, an IV in my arm, and a cage mask over my face to hold me perfectly still while loud, obnoxious sounds bang all around me. If that doesn't ease you on into an otherwise perfectly good Saturday morning, I don't know what does.

Lying stone still, I can't help but wonder what the images will look like. What story will they tell? As the radiologists help me out of the machine, I look for any "tells" in their facial expressions. Shoot, they're some of the best poker faces I've seen.

The ER doctor on call reviews the MRI slide images with us. He points out a golf ball–sized brain tumor nestled above my right ear. I try to absorb his words, but his speech quickly becomes muffled, as if I've been submerged under water. This is *my* MRI?

There's more, so I try to focus. It's an aggressive tumor; the doctor is quite sure it wasn't there six months ago. It's amazing how much one black-and-white image can tell those who know how to read it.

Deep cleansing breath in, slow calming breath out.

We are digesting information as fast as we can and filling in more details for the doctors. In utter disbelief, I'm confirming, "No, you won't find much of a medical file on me," and "My meds up until today have consisted of only a daily multivitamin and glucosamine. That's it. I've had no atrocious bump protruding above my right ear, no horrendous headaches, no vomiting."

Briefly snapping out of this medical nightmare, I remember we have a garage full of people slated to come over in just a few hours. Bob quickly places a phone call to Sharon Quast, someone who (a) can post a cancellation message on my Facebook invite and (b) has most attendees' phone numbers in the event they aren't on Facebook.

Miraculously, Sharon successfully reaches all but one of the invited couples. "Hey, where are you at?" a text dings in on my phone a couple of hours later. "We're outside your house and no one's here."

Yvette Zeece feels horrible to learn we are in the hospital, but I assure you not as bad as we feel having to unexpectedly cancel at the last minute. Let's just say there are days when life goes according to plan and days when it doesn't.

Within the next few hours, I am admitted to the hospital, settle into a room, and have a battery of vitals taken. Soon two surgeons of neurology are standing before us. They classify my tumor as a Glioblastoma–Grade 4—gut-wrenching words that no one is ever prepared to hear.

"We won't be doing a biopsy; we just need to get this d@#% thing out," the surgeon says.

I can sense the urgency when he asks when I had last eaten.

Bob asks questions about the tumor removal. "Is it something you just kind of scrape off?" he inquires.

The docs shake their heads. "No, you have to think of the tumor as soil and the brain as water."

Farm girl that I am, I get the analogy of tiny particles mixing into a liquid, but what an unnerving thought.

The surgeon proceeds to warn us there is a 50-50 chance

that the entire left side of my body could be partially if not fully paralyzed postsurgery. So now we're considering my arm and leg, not just my hand.

"Your tumor is lodged in the worst possible spot," the doctor continues. "It's right between your motor band and sensory band," he says, tapping the top of his head.

Next we ask how soon the surgery will be taking place.

"Definitely in the next day or two," he replies.

Breathe, I frantically remind myself. *You simply have to breathe.*

Time for another difficult call. "Mom, they want to do surgery in the next day or two," I weep.

"Kelly, I'm coming down there," she immediately responds. Not an easy task for a seventy-eight-year-old who lives two hours away and doesn't like to drive through Highway 7's roundabouts. "I'll send a text to your brothers and see who can drive me down."

Great, another not-so-easy task when taking into account it's October and my brothers are full-on with fall harvesting at Church Lake Farm. The absolute last thing I want to do is inconvenience anyone. First the Lutherans, now Mom and my brothers.

Jumping Ship

4

October 14, 2018

Midmorning my mother, two brothers, Lonnie and Ryan, sister-in-law Sarah, and nephew Brandon Fosso arrive at the hospital. Though a last-minute trip to the Cities is the *last* thing they expected to have on their list for today, you never could have guessed it. I am completely overwhelmed by their love.

Their early arrival leads me to believe that probably none of us slept well the night before. Mom arrives with a bag of dough-nuts and cookies in hand, of course. She also thoughtfully pulls out five or six small, framed family pictures that fit perfectly on my hospital window ledge. It is beyond comforting to have the whole gang here.

With not even so much as a mention of disrupting my broth-ers' busy harvest plans, my family starts absorbing how quickly this came on and the speed at which it needs to be dealt with.

Bob and I recap our surgeons' initial consultation for them. Then Ryan reveals all the internet research he completed on my behalf. He even reached out to his family doctor, Dr. Richard Wehseler, for guidance. It's clear Ryan knows far more than Bob or I do at this point and is able to jump right in and talk the talk.

We converse about the MRI slides we saw the previous afternoon, and I comment on how huge the golf ball–sized tumor appeared on-screen.

In textbook brotherly fashion, Ryan pipes up, "Yeah, but are you taking into consideration how small the actual brain is they're dealing with?"

Our tearful room erupts with laughter. It's the perfect sprinkling of humor we need at just the perfect time.

A nurse comes in to assess any changes in my condition. My symptoms seem to be progressing more quickly in the hospital than they did at home. By this time I'm having trouble touching my nose with my left hand. Since I'm unstable on my feet, the nurse secures a neon "Fall Risk" band around my wrist, and I'm not allowed to walk without assistance. The doctors put me on dexamethasone because the MRI showed brain swelling, and Keppra to keep any potential seizures at bay. It feels like everything is moving too fast, and soon we'll need to make decisions on surgery.

"It's certainly not my body, and I have zero reservations about this hospital," brother Lonnie expresses, "but when you have the best care in the world ninety miles away, have you thought about getting a second opinion at the Mayo?"

We tell him about our conversations with Dr. D, but from what we're hearing from the surgeons here, it doesn't sound as though we have time to wait.

Throughout the afternoon a steady stream of people arrive, including Bob's daughter, Lauren Blaisdell, and her one-year-old son, Paxton, who brings smiles to our faces. My room seems to have an ever-revolving door as more family members stop by, as well as old friends, new friends, church friends, high school friends, and couples friends. How beyond blessed we are to have so many people who care.

I receive a lighthearted call from Charlotte Christensen (aka Charo), a friend from Denmark. We met in 1982 when she was a foreign exchange student; over the decades she's become nothing less than a faraway sister. I also pray over the phone with Kevin and Diane Beuning from Arizona.

Simply by God's divine intervention, Amy Dornbach, a

close friend from high school, and her husband, Steve, just happen to be in the Cities for a long weekend away from their teaching obligations in Bulgaria. Their schedule is tight, she texts, but could they stop by? Amy and Lois Wallentine—another mutual lifelong friend—just happen to arrive at the hospital at the same time. It means so much to have both Lois and Amy by my side, holding hands, weeping, attempting to come to grips with such devastating news.

When the phone rings next, it's a call from Rev. Peter Geisendorfer-Lindgren, whom we haven't seen in more than two years since moving to the other edge of town: "Hey, I'm in the neighborhood. Are you up for some company? If so, can I stop by?"

Tearfully I give him my room number. Truly the Lutherans are out in force. In between every visitor, I receive exquisite floral arrangement after exquisite floral arrangement throughout the day. It's deeply humbling to say the least.

As the afternoon flies by, we reach out to our attorney friend, Joan Schulkers. We had met with Joan several months prior, to begin our estate planning process. We filled out forms and had many of our wishes noted; we just hadn't gotten around to filing it all yet. Now is the time. While it's an awful feeling to be getting your final affairs in order in the hospital—just days prior to having brain surgery—we consider ourselves fortunate to have as much completed as we do. Joan is just one more person who drops everything to come to our rescue. We will forever be grateful.

Numerous nurses are in and out of my room all day long for meds, vitals, and introductions after shift changes. That morning, when I felt as though I was getting worse by the hour, one enthusiastic nurse entered the room and exclaimed, "Kelly, you are doing so well! You are the only patient of mine on this floor who speaks today." Harsh reality.

When I look at the amount of care and compassion nurses possess, I jump to one conclusion: none of them are getting paid enough. I need help getting to the bathroom, showering, and moving from the bed to the chair and back again. Each time I stand up, a nurse secures a harness around my waist and holds on to me.

I thank Zhang, one of my ever-so-kind nurses, who became my protector overnight. Mom chimes in with her praise as well.

Without skipping a beat, he looks Mom in the eyes and, motioning to me with open hands, says, "Please know that just as you love her, we love her too." He finishes by tapping his heart.

Before one shift change, Kamau comes in to say goodbye, as he is scheduled to have the next few days off. "Kelly," he begins, "I heard the laughter. There was *so much love* in this room today. And these flowers! Where did they all come from?"

Teary-eyed, I know I am the luckiest girl alive.

My brothers and their families leave for home late in the afternoon. But soon a text arrives from my sister-in-law Sarah asking if she can set up a CaringBridge site for me. While it's surreal to think *I* need a site, it is becoming virtually impossible to keep up with all the calls and texts. I instantly recognize it will be a relief to Bob, who is fielding the vast majority of the calls.

The only words I can assemble for Sarah are "please" and "thank you"; I wipe away another tear.

During the course of the day, while enjoying our steady stream of visitors, Bob and I keep the idea of getting a second opinion wedged in the back of our minds. My symptoms now seem to be holding; the staff credits the dexamethasone, which is reducing my brain swelling. By evening I'm a bit steadier on my feet. We haven't seen the hospital surgeon again or received a surgery date yet, but more and more the Mayo consult feels like the right thing to do.

Bob reaches out to Dr. D for the names of her referrals. The first of the three responses she received came from Dr. Fredric Meyer, Mayo Clinic's professor of neurosurgery. Dr. Meyer has spent his entire career in this specialty field and is the current chair for the Department of Neurologic Surgery.

I guess there are days you have connections, and there are days you have connections. Bob leaves a message for Dr. Meyer, and we decide to check ourselves out of Methodist the next day.

October 15, 2018

The next morning Sarah returns to the hospital, this time with Emma, Elsa, and Harris in tow. What a breath of fresh air! The nieces and nephew run in with Happy Meals in hand, and I offer them the biggest hugs I can. At ages seven, five, and three, they are probably concerned and confused as to what cancer *looks* like. While I'm not at 100 percent, I am thrilled that a fairly normal Aunt Kelly can represent.

The checkout process at Methodist goes smoothly. The doctors keep me on the meds to prevent swelling and seizures, aware that we plan to have an appointment at Mayo within a day or two. Per hospital policy, an orderly pushes me out in a wheelchair. A few steps and I'm in the car.

As we proceed home to wait for a return call from Dr. Meyer, I think about a PBS documentary we watched about the Mayo Clinic approximately three weeks earlier titled *The Mayo Clinic: Faith – Hope – Science*. It was some of the best TV we'd seen in years.

One segment showcased a surgery performed on a violinist from the Minnesota Orchestra who was experiencing aggressive shaking in his right hand due to an essential tremor. To guide the surgeons as to where to insert wires to try and prevent the tremor, the musician played his violin during his brain surgery! Of course, at the time we had zero knowledge of my pending surgery. Boy, what a thing to chalk up to pure coincidence.

A Couple of Case Studies

October 16, 2018

Today Miracle #4 presents itself: we receive a return call from Dr. Meyer's nurse. He's had a cancellation and can see us for a consult tomorrow! What a blessing. My mom has opted to stay with us at least until we go to Mayo, so all three of us plan to make the familiar drive to Rochester.

October 17, 2018

We head out early as wc have places to go and people to see. Mayo doctors prefer to do their own tests instead of accepting outside results from other hospitals or clinics. So prior to our consult with Dr. Meyer, I have another MRI and more blood workup.

Then comes our first meeting with the neurosurgeon. While we were not uncomfortable with the care I received at Methodist, we are immediately *more* comfortable at Mayo.

"So how are you feeling?" Dr. Meyer asks as he looks me in the eyes.

We had learned from both Bob's POEMS syndrome experience and the PBS documentary that the Mayo Clinic takes a unique approach: their doctors treat the *patient*, not the disease. Quite frankly, it shows.

We tell Dr. Meyer what we know about the hazardous spot in which the tumor is lodged and the 50-50 chance of added paralysis during removal.

He validates what we'd heard about the severity of my glioblastoma, yet he immediately puts us at ease when he says, "I think I can pinpoint insertion from a different angle. I believe I can go in underneath your tumor, steering clear of your motor band. With that, there's only about a 5 percent chance of your left-side movement getting any worse."

While we realize no one can be certain of the results until I am off the operating room table, we instantly prefer Dr. Meyer's way of thinking.

The warm, wizard-looking professor of neurosurgery asks me to perform a few exercises similar to those I've done before: walk a straight line, stand on my heels, balance on my toes. He checks my knees for reflexes and my left hand for range of movement. Then he rolls his chair directly beside me and confirms that the meds the Methodist doctors put me on (anti-inflammation, antiseizure, and antinausea) are doing a great job.

After Dr. Meyer addresses all of our initial questions, we ask how soon he can perform surgery.

Opening up his calendar, he shakes his head and says, "My goodness, I have all this travel." (In addition to doing surgeries, Dr. Meyer also travels to Mayo Clinic facilities around the country to mentor fellow residents.) "October 30th is the first available date I have," he says.

"Now please keep in mind that I'm not you, but I honestly don't feel you're risking anything by waiting," Dr. Meyer reassures us. "However, if going home for twelve days to wait for surgery will keep you awake at night with worry, perhaps I should check my colleagues' calendars." He provides the names of two other Mayo neurosurgeons. "I assure you we don't have a schlep on our team," he jokes.

Sensing that a brain surgeon is something one should probably never bargain hunt for, we quickly settle on his care and solidify our date. And just like that, we have our Miracle #5: a plan, a date, and—the greatest gift of all—time to breathe.

Next we meet with Dr. Meyer's nurse, Paul Stuart. Paul is delighted to hear we chose to wait for Dr. Meyer.

"Dr. Meyer has an absolute *passion* for what he does," Paul explains. "You won't find a happier person in a pair of scrubs with a full day of surgery ahead of him than this guy." That compliment speaks volumes.

Paul unfolds the patient brochure and starts to explain every aspect of my upcoming surgery. He dots every *i* and crosses every *t*. Then he asks if I would consider being part of a case study. Not only does my quick tumor have an aggressive stage, but it's in a unique location.

If my participation might someday keep others from losing a loved one or friend, put me in, Coach. Already having one case study under our roof—Bob, for POEMS syndrome—we smirk as I sign on the dotted line. Now we're a *couple* of case studies. Whoa, what will the neighbors think?

We ask Paul what happens after surgery. While prefacing his response with several caveats, he gives us some rough predictions: one to two days in the ICU, then three to five days of recovery at St. Mary's Hospital. After that there may be a four-week brain-resting period before determining the path and logistics of chemo and radiation treatments.

Upon departure Paul says he will call soon with a date for my pre-op physical. Settling in our car, we are just exiting the parking garage as Paul's call comes through asking us to return the following Monday. He also inquires if we could possibly arrive the day before surgery so they can conduct two MRIs.

October 22, 2018

On pre-op physical day I strike up a conversation with my admitting nurse. She is amazed to learn (a) my diagnosis just happened October 13, (b) we were able to be seen by Dr. Meyer so quickly, and (c) we already have an October 30 surgery date.

All along this journey, it's easy to see the numerous small miracles falling into place. Armed with faith, hope, and an abundance of love, this farm girl is prepared to fight!

A few hours later comes the verdict: "You're healthy as a horse and cleared for surgery." No small coincidence here either, when Horse was the nickname my dad gave me growing up.

October 29, 2018

The day before surgery, I am back at Mayo for two MRIs. These will determine how easy or hard surgery is going to be. Eerily, there is a good chance Dr. Meyer wants me to be semi-awake during the estimated six-hour surgery. This would allow me to guide him by hand movements, letting him know just how close he could get to my motor band without causing further damage.

First is the specialized mapping MRI, charting my brain much like a GPS would. For the second procedure, they buckle me into a 7-Tesla MRI scanner as part of their case study. It's the only apparatus of its kind in the United States—less than a year at the Mayo Clinic. With its increased magnetic strength, this scanner provides very fine anatomic detail, helping radiologists see things that were previously invisible with other machines. I will say, that Tesla is a pretty sweet ride.

6

Go Time

October 30, 2018

Surgery day brings mixed emotions of both fear and relief. Ryan and Sarah are here. Lonnie hoped to come also, but someone has to hold down the fort; keep in mind it's still full-on fall at the farm.

Ryan and Sarah find an overnight stay for their three small kids before setting out on their four-hour, one-way drive. The last thing I want people to do is spend the entire day in either a car or a waiting room. But as much as I hate causing any inconvenience, it is an absolute blessing to have them here to support both Bob and my mom. I hadn't initially thought of that angle, but they clearly had.

I check into the preliminary pre-op room where nurses take more vitals. My family comes back and sits with me, as the staff isn't exactly sure how long it will take. I am the second surgery of the day. As edgy and apprehensive as I am to get this over with, I am so glad that Ryan insisted on being here. He's pure comic relief.

I leave my family at 10:00 a.m., reassured to know they will be receiving text updates throughout the day. Nurses will be filling them in on my status and whereabouts.

Go time, I think. *This is your time to shine*, I can hear Dr. Worley saying.

A little more presurgery prep takes place in a second room.

"Do you want to watch TV?" one nurse asks.

"We have music," another suggests.

The opportunity to shut my eyes, relax, and focus solely on

breathing is all my little heart desires. Careful not to get too far into my own head, I can't help but wonder if I will still be *me* in a few hours.

Putting my mind at ease, the anesthesiologist proceeds to place another feather in Dr. Meyer's cap. "I have to tell you," he begins, "you're under the care of the exact doctor I would request if my family or I would ever need to have this surgery done."

Rolling into the surgical room, I look up at a bright light the size of a small satellite dish above my head. I spot a large red digital clock before me reading 10:45 a.m. *Jesus, take the wheel*, I think as I drift off.

Next thing I know, I'm up in ICU where the clock reads somewhere after 6:00 p.m. *What an incredibly long day for my family*, I think.

My throat is sore from the oxygen tubes, but miraculously I have nothing more than a dull headache, so I ask for some Tylenol. I soon find out it may not be a headache at all; I have a gauze turban wrapped around my head that has to remain intact for two days. *Aha, that's the tight feeling*, I conclude. Eventually I seek out ice chips and some toast.

"Are you able to move your left hand?" the nurse inquires.

Slowly I lift my arm from my side, and I flex my hand just as I had done prior to going into surgery. This first hour in ICU they start a routine of fifteen simple exercises that they will ask me to perform every hour for twenty-four hours straight. They want to make sure (a) I continue to have movement and (b) that the message from my brain is getting to my extremities.

"We're going to let your family come in now if you're ready," my nurse says.

"Please," I reply.

Bob enters in at a little quicker pace than normal. Looking white as a ghost, he huddles along my bedside.

"Hi, honey, can you move your left hand?" he immediately asks.

Initially I take this as a rather odd just-out-of-major-brain-surgery question, but I would later understand why he asked. I show off my mad skills.

"Wow, that's really good," he replies.

A few minutes later, in come the rest of the troops. By this time, with all the long hospital halls to maneuver, Mom has agreed to use a wheelchair. What appears to be a not-so-big hospital on the outside has definitely become larger than life inside.

"What have you been doing all day?" I nosily ask.

"Oh, your brother and I took a tour of the hospital, and we found a nice quiet waiting room down by the chapel where we could all stretch out," Sarah offers, after glancing at Ryan. "Then we went to have a bite to eat."

For just having brain surgery, I am pleased the conversation feels relatively normal.

Nursing attendants are in and out of my room, but this post-surgery time with my family is priceless. I have made it through the eye of the storm, something I wasn't exactly sure would happen going in.

"Don't you think for a second Dad wasn't perched on Dr. Meyer's shoulder looking out for you today," Ryan reassures me.

Tearfully, I nod. Our father passed away fifteen years ago, and yet it seems like yesterday. Instantly I think of the framed words displayed on my bookcase at home: "Old as she was, she still missed her daddy sometimes." Today is undeniably one of those days.

After 8:00 p.m. Dr. Meyer enters my room with a smile and immediately asks how I'm feeling. I wasn't expecting to see him, so it's a pleasant surprise. Keep in mind he performed the surgery ahead of mine today, and he'll be getting on a plane early tomorrow to fly out to Mayo facilities in Arizona. He'll be teaching there and in Florida over the next ten days.

"I feel great," I say.

"Can you move your left hand?" he asks.

Sigh. *You and my husband definitely are cut from the same cloth*, my inner voice muses. After I perform most of the fifteen motor-skill tests, he flashes me another smile and says to the Fab Four seated in my room, "Well, family, that discussion we had earlier goes *right* out the window."

My ears perk up. I had assumed this was the first time my family had met with the doctor today. "Wait, you all have talked?" I ask.

"Yeah, he came and found us right after your surgery was done," Bob tentatively replies.

Jokingly, I look for a container of popcorn and settle in for the explanation.

Dr. Meyer had found my family after surgery. He entered their quiet waiting room with tears in his eyes. "I want you to know I did the best I could," he ever so sincerely conveyed. "I believe I got 95 percent of the tumor and came within three millimeters of the tumor's edge. Kelly's brain will be quite swollen after surgery, so if there's any movement on her left side at all tonight, it's a good sign."

Then came the kicker: "Kelly will likely need to stay in Rochester for three weeks of rehab to help her with her walking and/or left-side movement, as I don't believe she'll be able to get into a car," the good doctor relayed. "If she can pinch each individual left finger to the pad of her thumb, that will be amazing. Physical therapists can greatly build on those small movements." He paused for this to sink in, then suggested, "There's some time before you can see her, so I think it would be beneficial for you all to take a tour of our physical therapy area."

Rocked to their core, my family remained in complete silence for quite some time after Dr. Meyer left, simply trying to absorb his words. Bob sat motionless staring out the chapel window, which totally explained his ghostlike appearance once he entered my ICU room.

Ryan finally broke the silence and said, "Well, do we want to discuss the next steps, or should we go grab a bite to eat so we're ready to see Kelly when she's ready?"

Not having eaten all day, they made their way to the cafeteria. My brother knew Mom would be returning home with Bob and I whenever I got discharged, so he quietly cautioned her, "Mom, you need to keep an eye on Bob too. I worry about him."

Now hearing the details of Dr. Meyer's conversation with my family, I begin to realize just how very fortunate I have been today. No wonder after seeing my left-hand movement everyone was at a loss for words, even the good Dr. Meyer. He gracefully makes his exit, assuring us that his staff will be in close contact with him while he is away.

My nurse comes in close to 9:00 p.m. and asks if there is anything I want or need. Having been in bed close to twelve hours by this time, I ask, "My back is a bit stiff, so am I able to go for a walk?"

She grins. "I have to come with you, but boy, if you're up for it, sure."

We ever so slowly take two harnessed laps around the ICU floor, as other nurses stand smiling and clapping. "Can you believe she just had surgery today?" they say with excitement.

Late as it is, I encourage Bob and Mom to travel across the street and tuck themselves into their hotel beds. It has been such an incredibly long and stressful day for them.

"Don't be in a rush to get here in the morning, and have a

good breakfast," I command, knowing it is Bob's favorite meal of the day.

They depart, but I'm not quite ready to turn out the lights. Finding my phone, I answer a few texts and, of all things, get caught up on Words with Friends. Instantly a message chimes in from friend Jill Drees, with whom I've had a continual game going for years.

Knowing I was having surgery today, she messages, "OMG, I've never been so happy to see a game reply from anyone in my life."

By definition, a miracle is a surprising and welcome event that is not explicable by natural or scientific laws and is therefore considered to be the work of a divine agency. For all intents and purposes, a miracle is something I firmly believe happened today. Miracle #6 and counting. As I recite my prayers, I give God the glory. He definitely picked the right man for the job today. Ready for lights-out, I know I have been blessed.

There's No Place
Like Home

October 31, 2018

My first postsurgery MRI happens the next morning. The resident doctor stepping in for Dr. Meyer happily asks, "Are you ready for more good news?"

After reviewing the MRI, he is overjoyed to share that no remnants of a tumor exist! He certainly doesn't want to give false hope that a tumor won't return, because glioblastomas have outside particles or fingers that need to be continually closely watched. But at least for today my tumor is gone! Already the sun is shining brighter.

"Just for practical purposes, there'll be about three physical therapists in to see you today, but that's just our normal protocol," the resident doctor explains.

One by one, each therapist comes in, asks me to do a slightly different set of movements, then smiles, hands me a business card for future reference, and basically says, "Yeah, I've got nothin' for ya."

Finishing a late breakfast, I go out and about for another hallway stroll. Back at my room, I see Bob's sisters, Roxie and Linda, and his brother-in-law, Bill, have taken a road trip. It is so comforting to see them and catch up on busy lives. The more normalcy I soak in, the more tears magically appear. Despite not looking my best—don't forget that tight two-day turban—I am comforted to have visitors all the same. Good to see, and good to be seen.

Later, the resident doc makes his rounds. "I can't believe how well you're doing, Kelly," he exclaims. "We're going to get you into a regular room in a few hours, if that's okay." Music to my ears.

My nurse overhears that statement and pipes up, "I certainly hope that's the case, but St. Mary's is really full right now. Patients have been waiting *all day* to get into a regular room."

By 8:00 p.m. there's still no room assignment. I encourage Bob and Mom to head back to their hotel room so they can hopefully get a good night's rest.

After they leave, the resident doc appears again. He smiles awkwardly and says, "You're doing so well we can discharge you directly from ICU tomorrow morning and let you go home."

Thinking I didn't hear him right, I ask him to repeat himself. Home! I can hardly believe it.

I certainly hate to disturb Bob and Mom, but they need to know they should check out of the hotel earlier than planned, so I call. It's a good thing Bob is sitting down when I deliver the stunning news.

November 1, 2018
In the morning the nurses get me ready to exit, stage left. My turban still has to be on for a few more hours, so I inquire, "Are these stitches in my head dissolvable?"

"Let me pull up your chart and see; every patient is a little different," comes the reply. Much to my surprise, the nurse's answer is, "Um, no. You actually have forty-four staples in your head that need to come out in fourteen days."

All packed up, we depart with a trusty bag of new meds: refills of dexamethasone for brain swelling and Keppra to prohibit seizures, oxycodone for pain, and lorazepam and prochlorperazine maleate for nausea and vomiting. I also receive a supply of dapsone, a med I'll take daily once chemo begins.

Then we eagerly head for home. Bob picks us up in the valet

lane, where two kind volunteer attendants help both Mom and me into our vehicle. On the car dash, the time display reads 11:00 a.m. on the dot. *Miracle #7*, I think to myself: *we are departing a remarkable forty-eight hours and fifteen minutes after I was rolled into the operating room.*

Keeping with the theme, we arrive home to find our Miracle #8. Perched on our front covered porch is a beautiful arrangement of flowers sent by my nephew Trevor Fosso and his wife, Alicia. With no protective cellophane or paper covering, the bouquet has an attached envelope with my name, address, and a "deliver by" date of October 28. We headed to Rochester that day around noon and must have just missed the delivery. I can't imagine how those flowers survived our freezing, late fall Minnesota temps outside on the patio for five days. Uncovered. It's one of the most beautiful arrangements we received (and it would flourish close to fourteen additional days inside).

It feels so good to be home. Knowing I am in for a month-long brain-resting period, I crave a bit of quiet. While having my mom at my side has been wonderful, I know all the activity and worry have been taking a toll on her, so I encourage her to seek out a ride home.

I'm moving slowly, but I'm capable of getting around the house just fine. Another blessing in disguise? Bob works just four miles from our home. He is minutes away in the event I need to call him, putting all of our minds at ease.

Mom reaches out, and Sarah agrees to pick her up tomorrow. While grateful for the support, I'm now ready for some recovery time.

8

Head Hardware

November 2018

When I take off my turban, I see that Dr. Meyer had shaved only a tiny strip of hair for surgery. A row of perfectly aligned staples runs vertically above my right ear. It looks like I have a headband on, serving as just the perfect amount of bling for any occasion.

Resting comfortably at home, I soon welcome any visitors who are influenza- and otherwise germ-free. Perfect health for visitors is a must, the doctors stress, as my immune system is very low. With such a successful surgery behind me, I'm not about to take chances. Following doctor's orders is at the tippy-top of my list.

I wholeheartedly enjoy each visit from family, friends, and work colleagues. For many, life moves at warp speed, and face-to-face visits with friends are fewer and further between. So every visit is priceless, to say the least. The cards, meals, gas cards, girly spa items, ice cream, gift baskets, prayer shawls, and floral deliveries keep coming. Being on the receiving end of an abundance of compassion often brings me to tears.

Strangers, like Vi, reach out in kindness as well. A few days prior to surgery, I needed to make a transfer from our Charles Schwab savings account into our Klein Bank checking account. As this was a first-time transfer, I needed to do a penny deposit to confirm the money went into the correct account. For some reason, my initial attempt didn't work. Not wanting to trouble Bill Schwind, our regular financial consultant, I called Schwab's customer service number for assistance.

Vi patiently walked me through the process online, then asked if I could call back in a couple of days just to confirm whether the penny deposit worked.

"I'm sorry, I actually can't," I replied. "I'm going in for brain surgery, and I don't know how long I'll be in the hospital."

"Oh, I'm so sorry," she genuinely sympathized. "That shouldn't be a problem. I'm quite sure it will go through this time." End of our Schwab customer service conversation.

Now, a little over a week later, I receive a beautiful floral delivery with a get-well greeting from Vi at Charles Schwab. Knowing I had simply called an 800 number—and Vi's flowers were not at all associated with Bill's gift basket—my emotions erupt and I weep at the kindness of an absolute stranger. Sometimes miracles come in the form of kind people with amazing hearts.

In addition to flowers, an overwhelming amount of meals and goodies arrive. While I can make a mean PB&J, I'm no Betty Crocker. Just to set the record straight, I do own pots and pans; they just don't make an abundance of appearances. Oh, and a potato masher. I own a potato masher, but not for the same reason you probably own a potato masher. Mine happens to be for entertainment purposes. Like a great hunter setting a trap for her intended prey, I carefully open the utensil drawer, wedge the potato masher's handle in at both the top and bottom corners, and patiently wait for Bob to try to open it. Or better yet, I ask him to retrieve something in there for me. If that's not cheap entertainment, I don't know what is.

My mother—who still cooks for herself many times a week and sends bags of baked goodies home with anyone who will take them—must be mortified. Sorry, Mom. Evidently some genes skip a generation. For years I've viewed my KitchenAid mixer as a piece of countertop art and proudly display a refrigerator magnet received from my friend Lynnette Hubert that lightheartedly reads, "I have a kitchen because it came with the house."

Now suddenly my pantry and refrigerator are bursting with love in the form of food: tater tot hot dish, meat loaf, pot roast with potatoes, lasagna, pork chops, chicken and dressing, beef stew, chili, quesadillas, chicken noodle soup, banana bread, bars, and a better array of Christmas cookies than you'd find at Kowalski's Market.

Even in the mail comes a delicately wrapped box of our absolute favorite raspberry almond shortbread cookies from Leah Tiffany. Leah is a dear soul from across town whom we had recruited to make these tasty treats for us many times before.

Enclosed is a note that reads, "Kelly, if my memory serves me correctly, these were your favorite. I can't make them without thinking about you. Please enjoy!" Bob enjoys a couple too, but I quickly hide the rest for later.

There is also one Tuesday night angel named Michele who insists on bringing a warm meal to us for weeks and weeks—from the other end of town, after a full day's work, and long after we beg her not to. Clearly, everyone fears Bob will waste away to nothing without cooking help. Confidentially I can say he's never (ever) eaten so well in our lifetime. Funny, not funny.

In the mail I receive a bit of light Mayo Clinic reading in the form of a three-ring binder detailing everything you would ever want to know about a brain tumor. Before diving in, I ask myself just how educated I want to be. All sugarcoating aside, it's a scary disease. Glioblastoma brain cancer is an extremely severe, life-threatening disease. Not only is there no cure, but the tumor has roots. It's not something we fix and move on. Everyone who has this kind of tumor shares the same goal: to manage things the best we can for as long as we can.

Not a fan of taking more pills than necessary, I call the oncology line and ask the nurse about cutting back on the 500 mg of Keppra that I am taking twice a day. This drug is for combating seizures. Though many brain tumor patients have these, I'd never experienced one. The doctor agrees I can taper down under one condition: I must pay close attention to my body and report any slight changes.

A few days after cutting down to one pill a day, I begin to have an odd sensation on my left side. It feels like a million ants marching, starting in my left fingers and progressing up my arm, shoulder, neck, face, and left side of my skull. This happens about six to eight times a day. I obediently call in and learn it's a simple seizure called a Jacksonian March. Immediately I'm back to two Keppra a day, and—*viola!*—no more issues.

Fourteen days after surgery, I visit my local clinic to have my staples removed. All goes well, far better than a certain someone anticipated it might. Although I don't see the tool the nurse uses, it sounds like a nail clipper as it snaps each of the forty-four staples—and it feels like someone is pulling a few strands of my hair each time.

Coincidently, this nurse spent seven years working at Mayo. She confided that, in her opinion, the biggest difference between Mayo and every other hospital or clinic is that instead of focusing on the number of patients docs see each day, Mayo encourages their staff to take time out to teach, extend their learning, and hone their skills. With Dr. Meyer traveling around the country to teach other residents and Bob's Dr. D writing books on POEMS syndrome, we recognized this benefit as well.

November 23, 2018

Our next Mayo visit is on Black Friday. After an MRI, we meet with Dr. Michael Ruff, senior oncology consultant for Mayo's brain cancer care team. Subject on tap: radiation and which form(s) of chemo to use.

Dr. Ruff gives us the lay of the land: they believe they caught my brain tumor early, the surgery was a huge success, and interestingly enough, the tumor they removed via a vacuum was about 90 percent dead. Dr. Ruff finds this quite confusing and, when asked, admits he doesn't know whether it's a good thing or not. (Later, on our drive home, we decide to add it to the good column.)

Dr. Ruff also points out how fortunate I was to have the tumor above my right ear. Had it been above my left ear, it would have affected my speech and my ability to communicate, and it would have "changed who you are as a person," he explains.

Since my husband likes to know what makes things tick, Bob asks Dr. Ruff how Dr. Meyer obtained access to my brain through my skull. We are both surprised to learn I have a shiny, new trapdoor beneath my skin. At each corner of this rectangular door in my skull, Dr. Meyer added a metal plate with four screws holding each plate in place. New head hardware! Having previously spent twenty-four years working for W.R. Maleckar, a local manufacturers' rep firm that supplies medically implantable devices, I've actually held these screws in the palm of my hand. And should I ever quip about having a screw loose, please know how very true that may be.

Dr. Ruff explains that my chemo and radiation plan will be assertive. "Aggressive tumor equals aggressive treatment," he says.

Bob and I begin to notice that when Dr. Ruff talks about life expectancy, he speaks in months, not years. We shift uncomfortably in our chairs.

I'll receive two types of chemo simultaneously. While I will not be his first patient to undergo this, I'm not his twelfth either—so basically just a handful of people have tried this before. Both the aggressiveness of my tumor and the two-drug approach are the reasons Mayo asked me to be a case study.

After my first chemo cycle, I'll need to complete thirty rounds of radiation, going in for treatment every Monday through Friday for six weeks. We are happy to learn this can be administered locally. As much as we love the Mayo Clinic, we don't necessarily want to drive here every day.

During radiation, the medical team will keep a close eye on my blood counts. Dr. Ruff hints that hospital stays and IVs might be necessary. Again, due to the cancer's aggressive nature, it is important they treat it as aggressively as they can. We are okay with this and reaffirm our decision to let go and let God.

After radiation I will have about six more rounds of oral chemo—each being six days in length and approximately thirty to forty days apart—depending on how I tolerate it and where my blood work results fall. Whew, that sounds like a lot. Bob and I head home, heads spinning, trying to absorb all we've learned from Dr. Ruff.

Home for the
(Early) Holidays

9

December 2018

Early in December, I begin the chemo that needs to be completed before radiation. On Day 1 I take 210 mg of Gleostine, and on Days 2 through 6 I take 320 mg of temozolomide. This case study is off and running.

I quickly discover how my body reacts to chemo. First I experience about three days of zero appetite; after this period of water sipping, I'll semi-surface. Then I have a couple more days of exceedingly indecisive taste buds.

I spend hours on end trying to think of something that sounds even remotely appealing to eat. Sometimes it's odd food combinations. If Cheetos and chocolate pudding are what taste good tonight, Cheetos and chocolate pudding it is! Often what I thought sounded really good five minutes ago takes a completely different turn by the time we actually hop in the car and drive across town or briefly wait for our order to be delivered.

More than once I take a bite of something I thought I just had to have, only to wrap it up and bring it home for Bob's lunch the next day. I'm a fickle foodie at my finest. It's a road that's hard to understand unless you travel it yourself.

Nausea can strike without warning. If the pantry door happens to be open and I catch the smell of the wrong thing, it sends me into the bathroom gagging. Bob's danger zone while on chemo was cinnamon. Mine? One particular brand of tortilla chips we've enjoyed for years. Why I'm still two thumbs up on every other kind of tortilla chip (restaurant or otherwise), I have no idea, but this particular brand can place me in the fetal position. Just an idiosyncrasy that only a fellow chemo patient would understand.

Thankfully, the antinausea meds keep the majority of this at bay. These chemo side effects are not for the faint of heart.

With Christmas quickly approaching, Ryan suggests we switch it up and celebrate early this year, prior to radiation, while I'm still feeling fairly good. December 8 happens to work for all but one family member, so we mark our calendars.

Bob and I know this year is going to be a little different. First I suggest that we forgo putting up outside Christmas lights and instead just do a little something outside by our front door. Bob is already taking on the bulk of my household chores and errands; he undoubtedly has enough on his plate and I don't want to give him one more thing to worry about. Under duress he agrees.

Bob and a few friends offer their helping hands to set up our tree, but I simply don't have the heart for it this year. Scrooge-like as it seems, the fact is I already am not feeling great, and I don't expect to be feeling any better in early January when it's time to tear down everything. Regrettably, we cancel other holiday-related plans and decide not to send out Christmas greetings. My ever-present holiday guilt increases with every beautiful Christmas greeting we receive.

In the mail, I receive a folded-up letter from sister-in-law Sarah. She had been going through seven-year-old Emma's backpack and found a letter addressed to me. Reading it opens the floodgates:

> Dear Kelly,
>
> All I really want for Christmas is for you to get better. When I heard that you had a brain tumor with

cancer in it I couldn't resist crying all night. So, all I want for Christmas is for you to get better, that's all. <u>NO</u> toys no nothing except for you to get better. I really hope you get better soon.

    Love, Emma

For our early Christmas celebration, everyone from both sides of the family is able to make it except Bob's son, Danny Rodenberg. As a talented and busy contractor, he had been asked to work that day. Filling the house with laughter is Mom; brother Lonnie's family, including Penny, Brandon, Trevor, Alicia, and Kalley; brother Ryan's family, with Sarah, Emma, Elsa, and Harris; and Bob's daughter, Lauren, her husband, Andrew Blaisdell, and of course their cute-as-a-button son, Paxton. As Brandon reads the Christmas story, one-year-old Paxton sits at his feet looking up in wide-eyed, childlike wonderment. Before gift opening, sister-in-law Sarah puts her selfie stick to use and attempts to frame a Kodak moment for all seventeen of us. Between Mom not knowing *where* to look and kids not knowing *how* to look since everyone is laughing and joking around, it definitely is a moment to remember. Every Christmas celebration is fun, but this year's seems a bit more special. We just embrace the chance to all be together.

Ryan's plan to celebrate early proves to be his best idea yet, because on Christmas Eve and Christmas Day, I'm flat on my back, sick in bed. We aren't able to travel to the farm and attend the always-anticipated Christmas Eve service at the Old Mamrelund Lutheran Church, a stunning 1883 country church near Pennock, Minnesota, with its beautiful altar, freestanding church pews, rustic pump organ, and no running water, heat, or electricity. Generations of families attend the candlelight

Christmas services at Old Mamre every year, sometimes arriving by horse and buggy or snowmobile. It's the first time in more than thirty years that I'm missing my favorite part of Christmas.

My Church Pew Analogy

10

December 13, 2018–January 28, 2019

Six weeks of radiation therapy begins today. (Bless my ever-so-patient husband; he'll end up driving me to all but two of these thirty weekday appointments. I'm fortunate to have a list of volunteer backup drivers, and friends Lois Wallentine and Kelly Espy step in on the two days that Bob has a quality audit scheduled.)

Miracle #9 becomes easily recognizable on our daily trips to and from Methodist Hospital: Bob's relatively recent job in Chaska. Just five weeks before my diagnosis, a recruiter had contacted Bob out of the blue. At that time Bob was working in Elk River and was happy there. Being up-front, he told the recruiter he wasn't in the market to change jobs. But the more they talked, the more this position seemed like a good fit. The clincher came at the end of the conversation: Bob learned this position was in Chaska, four miles from our home versus the forty-four miles he had been driving. Without this job change, it wouldn't have been as easy for Bob to take me to appointments. While we may not always grasp it at the time, there's a Master Weaver who has His hand in absolutely everything.

At Park Nicollet Frauenshuh Cancer Center, Radiation Therapy, the technicians take precise head measurements so they know exactly how to focus the radiation at the area where my tumor had been. At each treatment, I lie down on the table and the techs position me by tugging an underlying sheet to the left or the right before I'm strapped down. They put my hair into a troll-type ponytail on top of my head and gently pull it through the top opening of my radiation mask.

The individually owned, perfectly molded, tight-fitting mask has an opening for my face, just from the bottom of my nose to the top of my eyebrows. The techs tilt my chin up or down; then they clamp the mask to the table with six clasps so I have no chance of moving my head. Radiologists tell me that even a misplaced hair under the mask can hinder the effectiveness of the treatment, so they take their time.

Finally, the team places a bolster beneath my knees, puts an oval foam ring that I can grasp on my belly, and slides me into the machine. It's precision at its finest. And in I go.

Thankfully, I have no issues with the tight quarters. If you're a claustrophobic-type person, I'm guessing you might. At this point all anyone can do is close their eyes and find their happy place.

And I'm out. Positioning me actually took longer than the radiation treatment itself.

The first two weeks of treatments go along quite nicely and at a good clip, but side effects begin to surface in week three. Radiologists warned me about the cumulative effect, and are they ever right. By far, the worst of it is the fatigue. There are days I think to myself, *Seriously? I'm supposed to get out of bed and brush my teeth today?*

Typically we farm girls rise early. But not now. It doesn't matter how late in the afternoon a phone call comes, it's certain to wake me up. I can't fathom how I am wasting all day in bed, but I have no choice. I begin to bargain with myself. If radiation is at 4:30 p.m., Bob will be home by 3:30. It's now 3:00, so I have until 3:15—or maybe 3:20 if I hurry—before I absolutely have to pry myself out from under the covers and get dressed. It's awful. Props to any fellow patients out there who can occasionally pull an all-dayer. I quickly learn you need to make the most of your good days and be kind to yourself on the bad days.

Also in week three I begin to lose a bit of hair. First to appear are a couple of small bald spots, one at the point of radiation above my right ear and another on the back of my head. For more than a month I am able to do a comb over, and no one really notices the difference. Eventually, toward the end of radiation, my scalp has a tingly, sunburn-like sensation.

Once a week I meet with the compassionate Dr. Robert Haselow. He is very familiar with the transfer of records to and from the Mayo Clinic, has a wonderful bedside manner, and never skips asking how my mental state is. Thinking his question odd, I quickly learn that radiation is a toughie. Depression is common, and oftentimes meds are prescribed. Thankfully, that is one pill I don't have to swallow.

I always try hard to look at things through someone else's eyes. *You never know what the person sitting next to you at church or work has gone through to get there that day*, I remind myself. As kids we're taught to have compassion, but retaining that into adulthood? Therein lies the trick.

My church pew analogy comes to mind as I sit alongside my fellow chemo clan in what I view as a far-too-busy waiting room. While this is not a place I pictured myself being just months after turning fifty-two, I also struggle to understand where all this cancer comes from. Breast, stomach, colon, blood, neck, throat, bladder, lung, liver, colorectal, ovarian, pancreatic—the cancer list is endless. In my own experience, I wonder if I'm hearing about this devastating disease more and more because it's in the news, affecting A-list individuals and friends of friends. Or do I notice it now simply because it also affects me? Whatever the reason, can we please just stop the insanity?

All we need to do is open our eyes and look around. I cross

paths daily with a gentleman in a FedEx jacket, stopping in for his late daytime appointments. *How is he working through these grueling treatments?* I wonder. I overhear another person undergoing radiation now for a second form of cancer. Unfortunately, lightning does strike twice. I start up a conversation with one woman who is navigating this diagnosis completely on her own. When she arrives home tonight, she has the stress of finding her next day's driver. Then I see an elderly couple lovingly holding hands on the bench and think how unfair it is for them to be spending their golden years in a radiation waiting room. Suddenly my particular tunnel seems less dark.

On my final day of radiation, the staff joyfully hands me a certificate of completion, which to me could just as well have been a four-year college degree. Most certainly I worked hard for it, paid for it, and best of all, received firsthand experience in life's ultimate class: Empathy 101. Now that, my friends, is what I call street smarts.

Head-Shave Day

11

End of January 2019

I am losing my hair more and more. Mine is *s-l-o-w-l-y* coming out in strands, unlike Bob's same-day fallout. He had four doses of chemo, two of which were lethal, and then received what I would call the benefit of waking up to clumps of hair all over his pillowcase one morning. The baldness decision was made for him, but I'll have to make the call myself.

Just as everybody is different, every *body* is different. Being blessed with thick hair may have slowed my baldness, but my hair is still deserting me over time. Having major fallout in the shower, I ball up any strands in my hands, flippantly toss them on the shower wall, and dispose of them in the trash upon exit so they won't clog the drain. Next I gently towel dry as well as blow dry my hair over the sink, wiping up hundreds of escapees. Keep in mind this is above and beyond what drops out on my clothes, furniture, and each of the twelve puzzles we complete this winter. *Ah-noy-ing.*

Cancer is a beast of a disease. It runs your energy tank down to well past empty, causes you to feel like crap, and makes you lose your hair all at the same time. Utterly relentless.

I ask Dr. Ruff how long the fallout might last. "Oh, I'm so sorry, Kelly, but another three months or so," he replies, as if he has any control over it.

I know my head-shaving time will come; it's just a matter of when.

When we start talking about it, Bob offers to shave his head too. I am speechless. This is a guy with a beautiful head of hair.

Prior to his own necessary cue ball status in 2012, I hardly saw him sport a baseball cap because he didn't want to mess up his hair. I hadn't offered to do the same while he was on chemo. His Johnny-on-the-spot offer speaks volumes of his love and solidarity. But long story short, by no means do I want him to shave his head; Minnesota is experiencing a cold spell, so I quickly issue him a pass. Rest assured, I will never forget that selfless offer of sacrifice.

While I've never felt like an overly vain person, let's face it, blonde hair is part of who I am. For us women, a buzz cut and head cover serve as the first visible sign to the world that there's something not quite right. Each time I decide to put it off a day or two longer gives me the short-lived feeling that I actually have an insignificant bit of control over an out-of-control diagnosis.

For whatever reason, the day I find a hair in my pancake syrup instantaneously becomes *my* head-shave day. I am now ready to enter the ranks of the Bald and the Beautiful! We happen to be at the farm, so I perch on a kitchen stool while Bob performs this monumental task. Mom makes a beeline for the living room because either she wants to give us privacy or it's too tough for her to watch. I'm not sure which.

My first reaction? Let me just say, most of y'all have no idea how much insulation hair provides. The winter chill has an extra bite for me this year.

Truth be told, I think the task is harder on Bob than it is on me. But we both know (a) in time it will grow back, and (b) in the grand scheme of things, this positively filters into our small stuff category. Glass-half-full person that I am, I set out to enjoy my much shorter showers and a whole lot less time at the salon.

Attacking the Floor

12

February 11, 2019

For two weeks I actually make it back to work full-time. Since November 2017 I have been working a dream job at the meteorological forecasting company DTN, where I am blessed with unbelievably kind colleagues. After four months away, I am more than eager to get back in the saddle. There is a welcome-back cake, beautiful flowers, an abundance of hugs, and even a few happy tears as I walk around to reintroduce myself.

The high of getting back to work lasts a total of nine working days. Upon arriving home on day nine, I enter our mudroom from the garage and suddenly find myself sprawled on the floor. I assume I caught my winter boot on the door casing. It is by no means a pretty fall; my entire left shin is bruised, and I'm sobbing. As a matter of fact, it isn't a fall at all. I attacked the floor. I threw my phone, emptied my purse, and flung my lunch bag into the laundry room. I'm sure people pay good money to see acrobatics like this. While I do perform all my own stunts, I don't always start them intentionally. Grateful I didn't break anything, I instantly realize just how far from red-cape worthy I am. Knowing Bob will be home in just a few minutes, I first allow myself a good cry, then proceed to call my mom. Sniff.

Comfortingly, she also suggests it could be the fault of my new winter boots and confirms that Bob will be home soon. After a bit more back-and-forth, making sure I'm okay, we hang up the phone. It takes me a moment to collect myself, but soon I remind myself just whose daughter I am and straighten my crown.

Bob arrives home a few minutes later and is stunned to hear what happened. Washing my face, I realize my pride has been hurt most of all. I allowed myself to feel down, but now I remind myself that I can't stay down. This is, after all, equally as scary for Bob as it is for me. Thankfully, we have a follow-up appointment at Mayo in just a few short days. And this time around, it can't come soon enough.

Winter in Minnesota

13

Late February 2019

Ah, winter in Minnesota. We're receiving record snowfall amounts in and around the Twin Cities. Our DIRECTV dish on top of our roof is evidently buried, as we've had no signal for about a week. Logging onto Facebook early Saturday morning, I learn that southern Minnesota (i.e., Rochester) is getting hit even worse than we are and will be closing all major highways beginning at 6:00 this evening. Great. We have an early Monday appointment at Mayo and had planned to leave Sunday. Gently I wake Bob and suggest we try to extend our hotel stay, pack up, and drive down today. Good thing we did.

The Mayo is an interesting place during a thirteen-plus-inch blizzard event. Our hotel lobby fills up with National Guard rescuers and stranded tourney families. Both the patient and employee populations are noticeably down when we check in at Mayo the next day. Considering how significant this appointment is, we're lucky we took the storm seriously. (We'll end up having to stay a day late as well, as the roads will still be closed.)

While in our hotel room across the street from Mayo, I experience two more falls. First, while stepping out of the shower, I catch my toe on the side of the tub and tumble. Then, while getting into bed, I somehow slide down in the small area between the side of the bed and the wall, scraping my upper left arm on the nightstand corner. I truly don't know if this fall is due to the slightly older, slanted hotel mattress, or if I wasn't situated far enough onto the middle of the bed. Either way, a huge bicep bruise appears. Not a huge bicep, a huge bicep bruise. Little did I know it would affect my upper left arm for months to come.

Neither of these falls are pretty either. Sobbing to Bob, I say, "It feels like I'm getting worse, even since we've been here." As it turns out, I am.

On Monday our own Dr. Ruff is stranded and can't make it in, but he's working from home and has reviewed my MRI results with his very competent colleague. The swelling in my brain has increased, which completely explains my recent less-than-graceful falls. He explains this is not uncommon given the short four-month period since surgery and the harsh treatments that have been applied (chemo, radiation, and additional meds). It just goes to show that time is relative. To the oncologists of the world it has *only* been four months, whereas in my mind it has been *four months.*

To decrease the brain swelling, Dr. Ruff recommends the medication Avastin, which can be administered at a local clinic via IV. My platelets are low as well, a catch-22 of being on chemo, so he suggests weekly blood draws to monitor my levels.

I ask Dr. Ruff if physical therapy could help improve my left-hand movement, but he suggests trying the IV first. "Let's walk before we run," he advises. In our instantaneous world, it is time for me to put on my patience pants. As I continue to count my blessings, being right-handed is definitely one of them. If I'd been left-handed, I would need to learn to write, eat, and type all over again.

Back from the Mayo, I take another next big step: I start looking for a wig. My close friend Diane Freeberg had been down the chemo and radiation path recently, so I ask where she got her goods.

When I set up my appointment, the consultant, Jan, encourages me to call my insurance company to see if any portion of the wig can be covered. "Usually they aren't," she confesses, "but every once in a while, I run into a case where they are."

I place a call to BCBS and find out that wigs purchased for alopecia conditions are covered; however, chemo and radiation wigs are not.

Before I overreact and give this innocent woman on the phone a piece of my mind, I take a deep breath and give her a piece of my heart. "Does that seem odd to you?" I inquire.

"Yes, it sure does," she responds. "After all, you didn't ask to lose your hair either."

The Wig Lady happens to be a cancer survivor herself; after her journey, she made it her mission to help other patients. Bob and I enter Jan's fourth-floor office and are astounded at the number of styles, colors, shapes, and lengths of synthetic hair. After trying on a few, I settle on the one that is closest to the hairstyle I wore preradiation. I didn't want something that screamed brand-new wig, as a wig itself is going to be an adjustment.

Come to find out, people who are really attached to their own hair can trim it, stick it in an envelope, and mail it to a place that makes human hair wigs. No separation anxiety there.

Surprisingly, there's a whole hair care line catering to synthetics: special shampoo, conditioner, hairspray, gel, a shine product, and shaping crème. Given that, I don't altogether understand when Jan advises me I'll be washing the nylon inside of the cap once a month and not the actual hair itself.

Jan then proceeds to caution me to be careful around ovens. Zero problem there, sunshine. Even the steam from draining noodles could disfigure my new do. Finally, I have a viable excuse to steer clear of the kitchen.

My husband, family, and friends are complimentary about what I've coined as my not-so-perfect wig. I think they're just trying to be nice. It's really a toss-up as to what comes off first when I walk through the door: my bra or my wig. Since my wig is the most accessible, it's usually the wig.

Everyone thinks it looks just like my own hair. Um, negative. To me it's slightly itchy, and it will take some serious bonding time to get used to it. Given the fact that my hair could take up to two years to grow back to a socially acceptable length, serious bonding time is exactly what I will have. Be careful what you wish for.

14

Normal around Here
Is Just a Setting on the Dryer

April 1 and onward, 2019

No joke, it's been a bumpy ride, this cancerous brain tumor thing. It has not only taken a toll on me, but also on Bob. He would be the absolute last person to admit it, but his life has changed immensely as well. Please don't think I've ever overlooked that. Outside of his day job, he is in charge of not only all the jobs at home he did before but also the ones I can no longer do. I know there are days when Bob is running on empty. I get the "Oh, but you've taken care of him" rationale and the "Kelly, he *wants* to" reasoning, but if you've ever been under the impression that there was only one of us battling this disease, you're sorely mistaken.

Just because I've been a caregiv*er* before doesn't mean that it has prepared me for being the caregiv*ee* now. It's hard to require help; it's hard to ask for help. From a young age we're taught how to do things on our own, to be independent. The instant the pendulum swings to the other side again, we feel really vulnerable. The upside to all this is that Bob and I have walked similar paths. Bob knows exactly what it's like to be knocked to your knees by chemo, have zero energy, surrender to a fickle appetite, and be fearful of reoccurrences. I don't expect needing help to get any easier, but I am learning my limits and learning to let go.

Due to this lazy left hand, things I can no longer control have taken an immediate back seat. Those who know and love my neat-freak habits would be amazed. Oh, everything still has its place, which is typically in a drawer, in a cabinet, or behind a closet door, but the dinner plates are no longer rotated for even usage, shirts and pants are hung slightly crooked on hangers, and beverage labels are no longer meticulously aligned. While I used to methodically sort our weekly wash into like colors and textures, I've turned over a new leaf and adapted Bob's longtime approach. Just call me "One Wash Wanda." I've also grown to understand that trash in a trash can is just as acceptable as dirty clothes in a hamper. Go figure. Funny how ridiculous these confessions look on paper, especially after you've been doing these things for years. News flash: life goes on. Lots of things are seen differently in the toughest of times.

Slowly we are focusing on getting back to life. We try hard to find hints of normalcy again, small as they may be. Some days it's mere glimpses of the way things were, the way *we* were. Other days it's sheer disbelief of the road we've traveled over the past few months. Perhaps the laundry room sign we've had for years sums it up best: "Normal around here is just a setting on the dryer."

For one who has forever planned in advance, I've become an absolute expert at winging it. Plans are now made chemo cycle to chemo cycle, MRI to MRI. Rarely past. Perhaps not everyone understands why my life has to be timed around treatments, but appreciatively most do. When friends talk about how great it would be to take a trip together in the next three to six months, for the first time ever I'm inclined to smile, nod, and say very little. Enjoyable as I know a trip would be, brain tumors and follow-up visits have a way of not letting you plan too far out.

Lately our plans are far from extravagant, but they are perfect all the same. Most road-trip weekends send us in the direction of either Rochester or the farm. Goals can be simply trying to get to church this weekend or taking a Saturday afternoon walk along a local path sans a parka. This *is* Minnesota after all.

Other people's reactions to my new normal have been . . . interesting. Most people fail to understand what the eye can't see. That's the thing with a brain tumor: you can't actually *see* it. No crutch, no cast, no wheelchair. The majority of the time I may look well but not feel well. If I'm having an extraordinarily bad day and happen to take a handicap spot because my balance is completely off or my legs feel as though they could collapse beneath me, not all individuals watching me in the parking lot are going to understand.

"You don't even *look* like you have a brain tumor." I've heard this a time or two, always said in an encouraging voice. I get it. No offense taken. Very few people know how to respond in terminal times. It's tough to be politically correct around those who have been slammed by a diagnosis with a lousy prognosis. *Inhale courage, exhale fear.*

I've found that some friends I once considered to be closest pull away, possibly fearful that glioblastomas may be contagious. Then some well-meaning people ask how I'm feeling but tend not to wait for the answer before inquiring about my upcoming weekend plans. That stumps me too. Others withdraw because they simply don't know what to say or do, and that's completely understandable too. I personally don't always know what to say either. Plain and simple, medical trauma can be awkward, even for adults.

The silver lining is that some people I've dearly missed have stepped back into my life. They mail intermittent hilarious cards, send check-in texts, or stop by with a gift card for ice cream. Not everyone stays—I *am* a lot to handle, after all—but know that the reconnection means the absolute world. This unexpected new norm isn't my first choice either.

There are no words for some moments. Like when a good farming friend of my dad and brothers looks me in the eye and tearfully tells me he's been praying for me. Or when Mom lets me know I am lifted up every Wednesday by her good friend's Bible study and still to this day remain on her church's prayer chain. With all my heart, I thank you, Butch Haug and Bonnie Rhoda.

So how do I deal with the occasional insensitive comment? Hopefully with grace. I remind myself that brain tumors are complicated and universally misunderstood. I certainly mis-read them prior to October 13, 2018. I choose to be gentle with myself when I contemplate having not only the most aggressive and elusive brain tumor to deal with, but the cancer too. I have days that are really, really good and other days when side effects bring me to my knees. Literally. I make a conscious choice to choose love as often as I can. And I praise God, thinking, *What if they hadn't found the tumor?*

"So, you're all okay now?" is a question I sometimes field. Truth is, I honestly don't know. Getting 95 percent of a tumor is a massive win, but this tumor has *roots*. It's not a marble that gets detached. Regrowth is a new and ever-present bullet to dodge. I'm learning that many survivors have multiple surgeries and multiple reoccurrences.

In general, people tend to like the short-and-sweet version of my story, not the really-what's-going-on version. We are, after all, a big-picture society. "While the surgeon did his best to remove the tumor that's visible, there is still no clear-cut cure. It's a terminal disease that I hope to beat," I explain. That's a tough response, I know. But while this glioblastoma is definitely a piece of me, it will never define me.

Recently I confided in some girlfriends that it was nice to have a conversation without mentioning the word *cancer*. While I completely understand the inquiries and appreciate the con-cern, it's sometimes just nice to get out of my normal day-to-day and be brought up to speed on how their busy lives are going.

Our days of entertaining have definitely taken a plunge. Party planning, one of my favorite things to do, has hit the back burner. We've thrown some good ones: a redneck deck party, bunco parties, murder mystery parties, casino parties, Bob's stem cell transplant party, card parties, house-warming parties, bridal shower parties, a friend's divorce party, a bon voyage party—you name it. To me, life in itself is a party. Suddenly now, all of our time and energy are focused on this brainiac party. Table for one, please.

Just recently I joined a few online support groups. While I thought about doing this earlier, it was one of those ideas that filtered in and filtered out. One private group is specifically for glioblastoma patients, one for tumors with humor, and one for cancer care in general. I quickly realized it was a good thing I waited a few months to join, or I may have freaked out. At the time of diagnosis, we were already flooded with information— definite analysis paralysis. Had I immediately become absorbed in other patients' stories, survival rates, and outcomes, I would have missed an important step in all this: navigating my own path.

I hate the fact that support groups like these even need to exist. Sadly, active membership numbers indicate there are far too many people like me. But I've since learned that I have an identical family out there. Is this headache normal? *Yep.* Does your scar feel funny? *Ten-four, little buddy.* I can feel my screws! *Whoa, cool, dude.* It is nice to ask the audience, use your 50-50, or phone a friend when necessary. While it was tough to click the Join button at first, I've discovered there is an abundance of kind people in this world. My heart breaks for every one. You learn, you empathize, you vent. We cooperate and graduate.

As I scroll through the comments now, I recognize the terminology, the medications, the statistics, the fear of the unknown. I begin to feel fortunate. Unlike other brain buddies, I never received news that my tumor was inoperable. I have yet to navigate a reoccurrence. The tumor, thankfully, was not in a place where it affected my vision. And I haven't experienced grand mal seizures, complete paralysis, or loss of speech.

Recently an online gal was having a really hard time with the thought of shaving her head. I tried to send comforting vibes, assuming she at least wasn't going to be bald in Minnesota in January. Little did I know, she was reaching out from Antarctica. It's probably not all rainbows and unicorns there either.

So I type with one hand and need to acclimate myself to not being able to do things as I once did. It's not even something I feel right complaining about at this point. If ever anything in these support groups becomes too negative or depressing for me, just as in real life, I keep on scrolling. It's certainly not impossible to beat glioblastomas, but the odds are just stacked against us. Finding your way through the emotional toll it takes is half the battle. What forever rings true is the enormous impact this disease has on spouses, parents, siblings, and children, as well as the patients themselves.

I find myself wondering if I'll be able to get back in the saddle—bike saddle, that is. My fear is that with this numb left hand, brakes may prove to be troublesome. Perhaps I'm putting too much thought into it. I was never good at stopping on roller skates either, but I still skated.

Bob and I have been fairly active pedal bikers over the years, logging a thousand miles in 2017. We loved finding new trails, planning our summers around beautiful cities and rides. We simply enjoyed that it was something we could get out and do together.

If you were to ask Bob whether he had a good time biking in Eveleth one year, he'd probably say with a twinkle in his eye,

"Well now, that *Depends*!" Months before, we had registered for the Great Energy Bike Tour with our friends Lee and Claudia Newman. Eveleth is 247 miles from home, and Bob realized a mere sixty minutes before go time that he forgot to pack his comfortable, padded biking shorts for our fifty-plus-mile ride that day. Feverishly, he did the only thing he could think to do. He ran across the parking lot and returned with two items in a blue, plastic Walmart bag: the only pair of men's spandex shorts they had and a much larger box of Depends, proclaiming "Ultimate Padding." Quickly stuffing the four-pack into his biking bag and heading to the starting line, he put his purchases to good use that day. At each extended water stop, we all laughed hysterically as he tried to discreetly head into a mini biffy and break out a new pair. And you wonder why I want to get back on a bike with this guy? Not only did he provide his wife and friends with some pretty cheeky conversation along the path, but he's been the butt of our jokes for years.

Over the years, I have been extremely fortunate to enjoy some great travel spots: Alaska; the Apostle Islands; Arizona; Aruba; the Bahamas; Cabo; Cancun; Colorado; Denmark (three times); Jamaica; Nashville; New York; Playa del Carmen; Puerto Vallarta; South Dakota; Tokyo; the magical hot air balloon festival in Galena, Illinois; the Bridges of Madison County and the Field of Dreams in Iowa; and the Kohler Spa in Kohler, Wisconsin, just to name a few. Focused on a very different trip of a lifetime now, this is one I feel fortunate to travel with Bob.

Bob frequently asks me how my left hand is feeling. From high on my left wrist and down, it's a cross between feeling numb and stiff at the same time. I equate it to that feeling when you're carrying too many plastic bags on one hand in from the car simply because you don't want to make a second trip. When I sit down, I actually have to watch where my hand is, as many times I don't feel if I catch it under a table or countertop. Worst of all, I don't always feel when Bob reaches out to hold my hand.

I've learned that living with a malignant brain tumor immediately puts things into perspective. What I thought was really important before probably isn't, and things I sometimes take for granted I really shouldn't. I've become abundantly more aware of precious, precious time. The absolute best advice I've been able to give myself is to lighten up, graciously extend olive branches whenever and wherever needed, and simply smile at the things I cannot change.

15

The Canary
in the Corner

April 8, 2019

At 7:55 a.m. we arrive for our next Mayo checkup. The Damon Ramp, one of two patient-only parking ramps, has six hundred of the eight hundred parking spots already filled. Keep in mind these parking spaces are for patients only. Mayo staff have told us that most employees park in superstore parking lots around the city and are bused in. You should expect to be a Mayo employee thirty-plus years before being moved to onsite parking.

As we wind our way to the top, Level 10, we play the license plate game: Arizona, Florida, Iowa, countless Minnesotas, Montana, North Carolina, North Dakota, Ohio, South Dakota, Wisconsin. Way too many sick people, I judge. On the elevator we strike up a conversation with a gentleman who has traveled seventeen hours by plane to get here. Even in his mind, the Mayo commute is worth it. All of a sudden our early alarm hardly seems like an inconvenience.

Included in each of our Mayo agendas is a list of dos and don'ts for the particular appointment: eat a low-fat meal/regular diet is fine/fast 12 hours prior; take your daily medications/skip your daily medications; clear liquids are fine/only take sips of water. Usually the list ends with, "Don't wear any heavy perfumes, cologne, or lotions to your appointment." Miss any one of these instructions and your intended Mayo day of testing could be in jeopardy. In our estimation the last instruction probably gets missed the most. When we are seated next to an offender, we silently think, *Oh, so that's why they spell it out.* Now I'm not saying the fragrances are *completely* overpowering, but I'm pretty sure the canary in the corner was alive before this person got here.

Just like most days at most clinics, the technician doing the blood draw struggles to find a good vein. Bruised and gun shy as I've become, my issue pales in comparison to the mother I see attempting to fill out her MRI form and soothe a fussing baby in a stroller simultaneously. *Where is she at in her journey?* I wonder. I pray she has caregiver support.

Anyone who has had an MRI knows it isn't the quietest of tests, earplugs and all. This scan will be number 10, I believe. Somehow I managed to fall asleep at my last scan. The cheerful technician rolled me out of the machine, exclaiming, "All done, Kelly!"

I asked if he could hear me snoozing from his little observation room. "No, but I'm surprised you could sleep; most people can't," he replied.

Instantly I flash back to my fourteen-hour Tokyo flight years ago. Having risen early for check-in, I somehow managed to fall asleep on the tarmac before takeoff. The young girl sitting next to me was amazed. "Wow, you're a really good sleeper," she said in disbelief.

Well, if you have to excel at something . . . , my inside voice thought.

We start out our afternoon Mayo consult on a positive vibe. Platelets are up and the brain swelling is down. Not only is a platelet transfusion unnecessary, but I can lessen my local blood draws to once a week.

Dr. Ruff hands me an Optune therapy brochure to review. "Now, this is not for everyone," he confides, "but it does have its advantages, and I want you to know it's out there."

In 2011 the FDA approved Optune therapy as a fourth

treatment for glioblastomas. This treatment involves no drugs or surgery; instead, it uses a helmet-like device that generates a low level of electrical current. The electrical fields slow or stop brain tumor cells from growing and dividing; they may also destroy the cancer cells. A patient would have many nickel-sized electrode patches attached to her head and wear the helmet for eighteen or more hours per day. Of course it can cause side effects, ranging from nausea and vomiting to seizures and depression. Already aware of this device and the level of commitment and side effects involved, Bob and I concur it is a big decision for a different day.

Sitting in our sixty-minute doctor consult with Dr. Ruff, we are again reminded of the amount of heart and soul he puts into his patients. Patiently and thoroughly he answers every one of the questions I had scribbled on my notepad, leaving no stone unturned.

"Kelly, I want to tell you you've been an absolute joy to work with," he relays. "We'll see you back in two months for another MRI."

Um, ditto, Doc; it's a date.

Choose to Live Life Anyway

April 13, 2019

Six months postdiagnosis and it feels like we've lived a lifetime since October 13, 2018. I've learned more about tumors, cancer, medications, and survival rates than I ever dreamed I might.

The past six months have been a roller coaster, with the highest of highs and lowest of lows. Prediagnosis, I usually felt pretty together. Postdiagnosis, I have days when I feel like my life has shattered. My focus now is on putting the pieces back together. Most of all I miss being able to make a plan and stick to it, even a simple routine in general.

Six months ago we heard the words "You have an aggressive brain tumor." We didn't altogether understand what that meant then, but we certainly do now. People in white coats tossed around terms like *glioblastoma*, *grade 4*, *neurology*, *oncology*, *radiation*, *chemotherapy*. We were advised there was no time for a biopsy; we just needed to get that "d@#% thing" out. After being further counseled, we figured out the words *glioblastoma* and *grade 4*, when placed together, are not nice words. We chose to live life anyway.

Six months ago I had an awake craniotomy. The thought of being awake while having my skull cut open seemed beyond scary, but we had every ounce of faith in Dr. Meyer, our top-notch surgeon. Some deep breaths and prayers, and we soon were at peace with the idea. During the surgery, upon his command, I moved my left hand as he was cutting out my tumor. This gave him insight on just how much of the tumor he could remove without further damaging my left side. Amazingly, I had no idea when or how long I was awake.

I had an abundance of worries about waking up post–brain surgery. Would I know Bob's name? Would I recognize my family? Would I still have all the wonderful memories of growing up on a farm? By the grace of God, I did.

The next few weeks at home I had to rest my brain. That's not too hard for a blonde, but it's still somewhat challenging given the multitasking world we live in. The docs wanted to keep the brain swelling to a minimum, so I played many Solitudes CDs and worked on beautiful puzzles. I had the comfort of knowing that Bob was working only four miles away should I need anything.

My staples came out easily, and the scary scar healed well. After radiation came a new hairdo. Never will I complain about blow dry time again. My baldness exposed a level of insecurity, as well as a feeling I hadn't felt in decades: self-consciousness. Yes, even at fifty-two.

Luckily, I haven't recognized any memory issues as a result of my glioblastoma. Asking for help is still hard. It's something we farm girls aren't used to. But I'm grateful for my helpmate.

I didn't volunteer for this role; I was chosen. I hope to defy the odds. For every sister or brother who joins me on this journey, it's not about how hard we fall; it's about standing back up. Oh, and that scar on my head? That's no imperfection. It's a badge of honor.

Optimism is a great healer and definitely the place where terminal illness will lose. While we have no control over the hand we're dealt, we do have control over how we react to it.

The Room of
Common Denominators

April 26–27, 2019

This weekend we are reminded why the Mayo Clinic is ranked Number 1 in the nation. As two spongelike attendees at their Brain Tumor Symposium, we soak up every ounce of information and inspiration we can.

Dr. Terri Armstrong from the National Institutes of Health in Bethesda, Maryland, opens the Friday evening event. Dr. Armstrong has been studying brain tumors for twenty-nine years and happens to be highly focused on glioblastomas in particular. A few enlightening takeaways:

- Glioblastomas are considered highly malignant.
- Glioblastoma cancer is an invisible disease that will be with you the rest of your life.
- Glioblastomas represent only 2 percent of all cancers in the United States.
- Eighty-two percent of glioblastoma patients are not able to return to work.
- A significant burden is placed on the caregiver.
- Patients can experience up to ten symptoms simultaneously.
- Neurosurgeons are faced with the decision of how much tumor can be removed without taking healthy brain tissue.
- Life now is viewed as *before* diagnosis and *after* diagnosis.

- From Day 1, your goal is to figure out how best to deal with uncertainty.
- Care team goals are to tailor treatment—what works for one will not work for all.
- Patients need to focus on what they *can* do rather than on what they *can't* do.

The symposium is a packed house of approximately one hundred patients and caregivers, inevitably something the presenters are both glad and sad to see. While we have unique stories of how we got here, ultimately we all have a common denominator. There's so much to appreciate being in a room full of people who are going through the exact same thing you are at the exact same time. We rub elbows with fellow warriors who have scars, caps, turbans, and the Optune therapy apparatus I've been researching, and this gives me a sense of comfort that I'm not alone. These are definitely some of the most courageous people around.

The entire Mayo staff seems excited about this rare patient symposium. "Usually we're talking geek to geek," one surgeon explains. "The ones we *really* like to hear from are the patients. It's only in places like this where we get to hear what our patients are expecting."

One of his scenarios hits home. The surgeon continues, "If, for instance, you think the first MRI postradiation will show your tumor as being noticeably smaller after all those treatments, we need to better coach you on what to expect and hopefully avoid the disappointment. Almost always brain swelling or edema is visible after radiation."

Um, guilty as charged. I went to my first post-op MRI consult with the attitude that the scan had better be improved since the radiation treatments tore me down the way they did.

Instead, my MRI showed additional swelling, explaining why I experienced three falls just days prior to the scan.

It's no mystery why medical school takes the length of time it does. With brain tumor names like AA3, astrocytoma, craniopharyngioma, ependymoma, germinoma, glioblastoma, medulloblastoma, meningioma, neuroblastoma, oligodendroglioma, and schwannoma, I'd be held back simply due to mispronunciations. There are so many tumors to choose from, and my Glioblastoma–Grade 4 (GBM4) is the baddest of the bad. In case there's ever a question, I do not like a tumor here or there; I do not like a tumor anywhere.

The doctors also joke among themselves about not having a clue why the majority of brain tumors are associated with fruit: plum-sized, pear-sized, apple-sized, grapefruit-sized. Only on rare occasion do they hear of one being walnut-sized or, like mine, golf ball–sized. Maybe it's a Minnesota thing.

By far the most touching speech comes from Dr. David Daniels, who specializes in pediatric tumors. Many times along this journey I've wondered how parents might attempt to explain brain cancer to their children, whether the patient is an adult or child. Why do they feel as horrible as they do? Why has the word *chemo* entered their vocabulary? Why can't they attend school or run outside and play like their friends?

Dr. Daniels opens by explaining how deep of a bond the doctor-patient relationship can be—so much so that he slightly upset his wife this morning, informing her that he would be going directly from speaking at our Saturday symposium back to the operating room. A young patient—who has only been under his care—is experiencing minor postsurgery complications.

Looking at his watch, Dr. Daniels remarks, "He and his family should be arriving right about now."

Instantly I flash back to Dr. Meyer's teary-eyed conversation with my family right after surgery, indicating that he'd done the best he could. To have such heart.

Dr. Daniels clearly feels blessed to have found his calling. Yet as a dad of three beautiful kids, he admits there are days he's found himself crying in a stairwell after a particularly tough consult. He confesses to frequently convincing his son to drop the electronic devices and play catch with him in the yard.

We're seated next to a gentleman and his caregiving wife from Fergus Falls. Coincidentally, he not only has a GBM4 but he is also under the care of our favorite Dr. Meyer. While I'm pleased to talk to someone who has been down my identical path, I'm more pleased to see him doing well three years later. Absolutely nothing feels strange about diving into conversations about the shock of diagnosis, similar medications, successful and not-so-successful therapies, and tearful caregiver conversations. His initial symptoms were seizures; mine was an uncooperative left hand. I am thrilled to learn that he is in a pattern of Avastin IVs every two weeks and follow-up MRIs every two to three months. His lingering effects include being a bit tongue-tied and not thinking quite as quickly as he used to.

In hindsight my GBM4 journey has probably been relatively easier because things did move quickly. Many patients are faced with *months* of testing, decision making, and option weighing. At each step in my treatment, I heard, "This is what we need to do . . . ," and "probably sooner versus later." Granted, the final decision is and always was mine, but who am I to question the utmost qualified?

Hats off to the mighty Mayo for passionately sharing such wonderful insight.

Symptoms Based on Brain Tumor Location

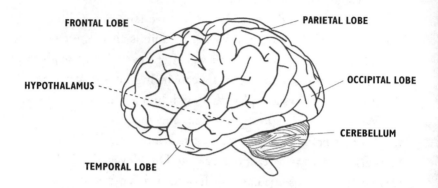

Frontal Lobe

Weakness
Paralysis on one side of body
Mood disturbances
Difficulty thinking
Confusion
Disorientation
Mood swings

Hypothalamus

Emotional changes
Deficits in perception
  of temperature
Problems with growth/
  nutrition (in children)

Temporal Lobe

Seizures
Perceptual/spatial
  disturbances
Inability to understand
  multi-step commands
  (receptive aphasia)

Parietal Lobe

Seizures
Paralysis
Problems with handwriting
Mathematical difficulty
Motor skill deficits
Loss of sense of touch

Occipital Lobe

Loss of vision

Visual hallucinations

Seizures

Cerebellum

Loss of balance (ataxia)

Loss of coordination

Headaches

Vomiting

Dizziness

The list of symptoms is from *Barrow Brain Tumor Handbook* (Phoenix, AZ: Barrow Neurological Institute, 2018), 13, https://www.barrow neuro.org/wp-content/uploads/BrainTumor_Handbook_Rev_11-18.pdf.

Fifty Shades of Gray

May 2019

May is Brain Tumor Awareness month! My support group sites are filled with encouraging messages, summer 5Ks scheduled across the country, gray ribbons, and catchy slogans and hashtags, such as "No One Fights Alone," #GoGrayinMay, and #GrayMatters.

When we moved a couple of years ago, we decorated our home in gray. I'm pretty sure we did this simply because it was the fashionable color at the time rather than a vision of things to come. But as we all know, God does work in mysterious ways. Thankfully, I love gray. We probably have fifty shades of gray—walls, window coverings, carpet, blankets, countertops, accessories, area rugs, floor tile, shower tile, patio furniture—you name it. One can't look far and not be brain tumor mindful in our home.

Where do brain tumors come from? That's an elusive question. I've read a few articles hinting at cell phone radiation. In today's world it probably makes sense. For some cancer fighters it may even make sense. However, glioblastomas have been around far longer than cell phones (1926 vs. 1973), and I can tell you this is not the cause of my tumor. Rarely do I use my cell phone, and when I do, the majority of time it's on speaker.

At diagnosis, patients and loved ones sometimes have to make quick decisions regarding something they know little to nothing about. Treatment must be placed in motion, as glioblastomas grow very rapidly if left untreated. Your skilled surgeon removes as much as possible without jeopardizing your quality of life. I'm honestly not altogether sure who has the tougher job—the docs, patients, or loved ones—but what a prime example of putting your life in other people's hands.

In my experience, individuals with terminal brain tumors tend to live on an ever-present edge. We hope and pray to hear the words, "Good news," from our oncologists, yet there's always the fear of getting a look, having a gut feeling, or having the good news slip backward into a hard conversation that indicates otherwise. Long gone are the days of feeling like I'm out of the woods. Now the slightest change in my balance, an involuntary twitch of my left hand, and every dropped item makes me think it's a neurological change rather than just being clumsy. Little things like that can push your emotions to the limit.

Should I be fortunate enough during a checkup to hear comments like "no new growth," "stable," or "unchanging," I unquestionably exhale a huge sigh of relief. In my mind I'm not quite thinking *safe*, but *safe for now*.

I simply love to hear stories of long-term glioblastoma survivors who technically shouldn't be here. They are my ray of hope, my courage, my bundle of sunshine. Statistically speaking, only 10 percent of individuals with this disease survive five years. Not stellar by any means. What I choose to focus on is the fact that I had one of the best neurosurgeons in the country, Dr. Meyer, who was able to remove 95 percent of my tumor. What I need to let sink in is that reoccurrence is not only possible but probable. That's where the *safe for now* piece comes in. I'm quite sure that long-term survivors have to live with some inconveniences, but for now they are my heroes.

I'm unbelievably fortunate to have so many people in my corner. Sadly, that's not the case for everyone. Who helps them with all of this overwhelming paperwork? Who sorts their pills if they are unable? Who wipes away their tears? I'm deeply humbled every time I hear or read, "You're an inspiration," "Keep fighting, farm girl," or #Godsgotkelly.

Never one to shy away from new friendships, I find myself keeping somewhat of a tighter circle these days. Not only do I want to avoid telling newcomers what I'm going through, but it's hard to keep explaining why life needs to revolve around chemo cycles, MRIs, and Mayo trips. When not appearing sick, I certainly don't expect others to understand that I've embarked on the fight of my life against an unforgiving brain tumor *and* cancer. The ultimate BOGO (buy one, get one), I guess.

We've shaved three-fourths of my head four times now, attempting to keep it at relatively the same length. I've reverted to using Johnson's Baby Shampoo—no more tears! *Falser than false advertising*, I think to myself, knowing full well that every single chemo patient out there has cried in the shower at least once.

When I hold up a purple pocket mirror in the bathroom, I can see that my once ear-to-ear bald spot is slowing filling in, with the exception of the patch above my right ear—the tumor site that received targeted radiation. If I look *real* close in the mirror, some days I see a bit of five o'clock shadow in this area. Woohoo! Other days I'm sure it's wishful thinking. Per the literature I've read, hair sometimes takes years to grow back in these areas. But hey, isn't shaving your hair on one side also a style? Maybe I'll be punk.

For now I will allow turbans, newsboy hats, and a not-so-perfect wig to be a piece of me. Just don't be startled if you ever catch me on a no-hair-don't-care day. And I'll keep cheering on my five o'clock shadow. A valuable thing I've learned throughout this process is that each victory is worth celebrating, no matter how great or small.

Thankfully, my fellow cancer warriors have a recent victory

to celebrate as well: Airbnb announced a strategic partnership with the Cancer Support Community. Through this collaboration, the Airbnb community will provide free housing for cancer patients and caregivers, provided they meet certain geographic and income criteria. This development is major for any cancer patients traveling from a distance to their treatment centers. From the press release:

> The Cancer Support Community fields thousands of calls from individuals who are struggling to cover the cost of traveling for treatments, scans, clinical trials, and other medically necessary care. This grant from Airbnb is a game-changer for these patients and caregivers—and you can hear the relief and gratitude in their voices as they learn about the free housing from the Airbnb community.*

A little insider support-group feedback:

- "This is a very beautiful thing! We travel two hours from home three times a week."
- "How nice! I travel over a hundred miles. After ten days of radiation, sometimes it's too painful to make it home in a back brace."
- "This is amazing. You have no idea how much it means to me. I lost my husband to cancer. This is one less thing I'll have to worry about when it's necessary that I travel for treatment."

---

* Kim Thiboldeaux, CEO, Cancer Support Community, "Free Housing for Patients Traveling for Cancer Treatment," Cancer Support Community, www.cancersupportcommunity.org/airbnb.

- "Unbelievable! We have had to get full price lodging when the Ronald McDonald House was full. It's been a huge financial burden."

Also in early May, about eight of the advocates who put on the Mayo symposium made their way to Capitol Hill. Backed by patients, researchers, and advocates, they hoped to make the most of their lobbying experience, as well as ask for funding. Their big ask for billions of dollars in research money for the National Institutes of Health and National Cancer Institute may seem out of reach. But in the last hundred years there have been only four approved drugs and one device to help those of us with the disease. They knew it was the right fight.

The shocking point they tried to convey to Congress is that glioblastoma is a disease that everyone should care about; it's the most common and deadliest malignant brain tumor in adults. It can strike men, women, and children of any age, background, or walk of life. It does not discriminate between gender, economic status, region, age, or political party. Our patient population is in desperate need of new and better treatment options. There is no cure and few effective therapies, and survival rates for this disease remain unacceptably low. Sadly enough, there's not enough *gray matter* involved in research.

Somewhat recently, glioblastomas are getting faces attached to their name—including Beau Biden, Senator Ted Kennedy, Senator John McCain, and local to Minneapolis, Denise Rosen. Everyone seems to be thinking outside the box. Pharmacies and other companies are rallying to support cancer patients. CVS Health has committed $10 million to the American Cancer Society for research, offers patient services, such as free transportation and lodging near hospitals, and provides tobacco-free incentives. Rite Aid partnered with the Skin Cancer Foundation to give clients free, full-body skin cancer screenings out of a roving RV traveling across the country. Great Clips salons provide complimentary clipper cuts to customers facing hair loss due to cancer treatments, as part of its Clips of Kindness program. Walgreens' Feel More Like You program offers patients consultations with beauty specialists who know how to conquer the physical changes that accompany cancer treatment. After all, looking good is part of feeling good.

I recently viewed some TEDx Talks on YouTube. Dr. Christopher Duma is a neurosurgeon specialist whose talk is called "Leading-Edge Pinpoint Radiation Technique."* Including residency, he is in his thirtieth year of glioblastoma treatment and study. He says the success rate for treating GBMs has not improved in those thirty years.

Glioblastomas are highly invasive tumors that do not grow in the typical snowball fashion—adding cells and getting larger and larger, like every other tumor in the body does. Instead, GBMs are multifocal tumors that can be found in many places at once. Remove it initially over here, and it could resurface over there. Don't treat the tumor at all, and your life expectancy is a few short months.

The way Dr. Duma explains the human brain, it is like a bowl of Jell-O with plastic wrap around it. The plastic wrap–like layer just helps the brain hold its shape. A regular tumor would be like a strawberry inside the Jell-O; regular tumors are hard and contained. They can be easily removed, and the brain would come back together. But with GBMs, the tumor doesn't have firm edges or a shape; it is also the consistency of Jell-O and infiltrates

* Christopher Duma, MD, "Leading-Edge Pinpoint Radiation Technique on Glioblastoma," May 3, 2016, https://youtu.be /hErXkeIadsY.

the brain. Moreover, the tumor cells spread by traveling white matter "highways" from one area of the brain to another.

Since glioblastoma growth is so dramatic, Dr. Duma concentrates on trying to outsmart it. He asks which of the highways in the brain it will move to next. What once I imagined as a round tumor is actually more like hundreds of thousands of amoebas looking to squeeze their way onto the next road.

After a six-year patent process, Dr. Duma has introduced a Gamma Knife procedure of pinpointed radiation. His concept is to treat not only where the tumor *started* but also where it is *going*. His treatment cuts the tumor off at the pass, much like firefighters do to prevent forest fires from spreading. He quotes Wayne Gretzky: "Go where the puck is going, not where it has been." And his results show impressive survival rates for people in his study, even up to twelve years. Absolutely remarkable.

Coincidentally, my nephew, Brandon Fosso, is also involved in research that impacts cancer treatment. As a software engineer, he works on programs that aid medical professionals in assessing changes in tumors. Lately, his work has focused on MRI images of—you guessed it—glioblastomas. Essentially, the software takes MRI images from before and after treatment and uses complex calculations to compare the scans. Doctors receive color-coded maps showing where things have improved, worsened, or stayed the same. Presently, the program is used for research, but the developers hope to widen its use one day. Brandon thoroughly enjoys working in this exciting field where there is so much opportunity to help cancer patients.

On May 11, at the urging of the Mayo Clinic lobbyists, a bipartisan group of senators proposed a resolution to make Wednesday, July 17, 2019, Glioblastoma Awareness Day. Here's to raising more awareness, advancing medical treatments, and celebrating more victories for patients and their families.

So What's Your Prognosis?

May 13, 2019

Tough realization today. Just like 82 percent of the other glio-blastoma patients, I may not be returning to work. As I drive to my Social Security appointment at the local Bloomington office, I think of all the now vital acronyms I hadn't given a thought to seven months prior: STD (short-term disability), LTD (long-term disability), SSDI (Social Security Disability Insurance), and more. This journey has been an educational one to say the least. Yeah, *that's* it, "educational."

Arriving a few minutes ahead of schedule, I allow myself to breathe in the parking lot and temporarily mourn leaving DTN—the exciting, growing company with the picture-perfect executive assistant job I was blessed to work at just prior to this darn diagnosis. I'll especially miss my creative colleagues; far more than your average eight-to-five coworkers, these are some really, really outstanding people. Always loving my profession, I told Bob and our financial adviser a couple of months ago that I'd like to work on the longer versus shorter side of retirement. The best-laid plans . . .

Sensing it probably isn't a good idea to walk into a 9:00 a.m. appointment all teary-eyed, I grab a tissue and check myself in the rearview mirror before I proceed to open the door of the Social Security office. *This visit seems to be about ten years too soon and for an entirely different purpose than I intended*, I think to myself.

Just inside the door is a ticketed check-in line filled with individuals who all have had a prognosis, a disability, a story.

Guaranteed, every one of them is aware that life can—and will—change on a dime.

The PA system invites me back for my interview at window #9. With a folder chock-full of medical business cards, pertinent dates, current medications, personal information, and partially completed paperwork, I'm delighted to be assigned to one of the cheery associates.

"So what brings you in?" she asks.

I recap my recent death-defying cancer battle in twenty minutes or less without giving the impression that there's a black cloud hanging over my head. No small task when you're asked to explain your up-close-and-personal connection with a terminal disease.

We start at the beginning: symptoms, diagnosis, tumor name, grade, clinics, and hospitals. Then comes the all-too-familiar, million-dollar question: "So what's your prognosis?"

Crickets. *Boy, if I had a nickel for every time I've been asked that*, my inside voice murmurs.

Attempting to enhance my earlier explanation, I decide to dive right in: "Glioblastomas are the worst form of brain cancer, and a grade 4 malignant tumor is the worst grade of the worst tumor. They spread quickly and are difficult to treat. Even if the visible part of the tumor is entirely removed, regrowth is a constant factor because the tumor sends out fingerlike tentacles that worm their way into surrounding brain tissue. The exact cause of the disease remains unknown. The median survival expectancy is not great, but I like to think I'm slightly above average," I say with a smirk.

The entire time her fingers are typing *clickity-clack*. I envy her speed. *Me and my sole-working right hand don't stand a chance anymore*, I muse. It's odd how suddenly a profession you've thoroughly enjoyed your entire life can be out of reach.

Within a matter of minutes, she asks, "Do you have anything else to add? We're about done here."

While she certainly received the short version of my story, I feel like I've covered the bases.

Before my appointment, several people advised me that due to the terminal nature of the disease, GBM4 patients are pushed to the top of the list. Instead of the standard five-month waiting period to go on disability (which had passed already anyway), I should expect a determination in two to four weeks.

Today's Social Security rep kindheartedly explains she cannot make the determination herself. "All of your information needs to be input. At the end of our interview, the computer will tell me whether or not you are a candidate who can bypass the standard waiting period."

With the push of her final keystroke, she quietly leans over the desk and confirms, "Yes, you're flagged. The waiting period will not be a long one."

No pomp, no circumstance. No going away party. Just a weird out-of-body experience of being forced into early retirement. It's one more step in life I wasn't prepared to take, but I check it off the list all the same. A mere four days later, there's an SSDI deposit in our account.

Taking It All in Stride

May 20, 2019

Since the soundtrack for life apparently has no indicative scary background music associated with brain tumors, I never know at what point in time things may change. Because of this, I'm on a mission to encourage Bob to form additional/closer male friendships. Let's face it, ladies, in a relationship, the majority of activities are done with *our* family, *our* friends, and *our* hand-picked couples.

Nothing about the current state of me has been easy. Yet Bob has taken it all in stride. He patiently understands why my movements have slowed, realizes that going places now takes us longer, and even ever-so-patiently cuts any food I need help with since I can no longer hold a fork *and* a knife. It's not surprising. He's also the guy who moved in with his father after dementia warranted it. Bob looked after his dad for three years, patiently bathing him, fending off scam callers, paying bills, sorting meds, taking him to appointments, and cooking meals.

In recent years Bob took a break from golf. (Okay, maybe it was due to the three rotator cuff surgeries.) Now I'm thrilled to see him going out on nice nights to hit a few golf balls at our neighboring Chaska Town Course. I've also encouraged him to take up some card playing or to check out our local Chanhassen AutoPlex again. The AutoPlex is a private garage condo community where 120 owners use their spaces to store, showcase, and restore their collector, classic, and exotic cars and motorcycles. He just loves looking at that kind of stuff. Just like the pretakeoff airplane safety announcement says, it's important for Bob to put his own oxygen mask on before assisting others. Anywhere that's enjoyable for him to hang out is just ducky with me.

In addition to being concerned about Bob, I am guilt ridden about not keeping up with friends. I probably have a friend or two who feel as though I've ghosted them. Please know it's not you; it's me. It's hard to be reminded of all the wonderful things we once enjoyed together. Fatigue and low energy remain very big factors until I'm out from under this chemo cloud. I fear not being able to keep a date and, maybe worse, not being very enjoyable on that date. And I certainly don't expect anyone to come over and sing "Kumbaya" with me. I need to spend my energy bank wisely.

When my tears come now, it's usually when I'm sitting at the laptop writing my way through this, or at night when I'm pretending to be asleep. Deep down I'm just a girl who's scared.

Precious, Precious Moments

May 24–27, 2019

Just past the effects of this month's chemo crud—cycle #4—I'm elated to realize I'm feeling well enough to keep our reservation and head up north for a couple of days over Memorial Day weekend. It's our first getaway since Labor Day 2018.

Like radiation, chemo has a cumulative effect as well. And let me just say, the snowballing is horrible. In the earlier cycles I'd have three to five days of mostly sleeping, no appetite, and bone aches. By cycle #4, it's ten to twelve days of downtime, undeniably time for the big girl panties. It's tough when you feel like an absolute shell of your former self.

The worst part for me is not knowing from day to day how I'm going to feel. Regrettably, I still have three more cycles to go. *I think I can, I'm pretty sure I can, I know I can.* If one form of chemotherapy has a way of all but killing you before making you better, perhaps you can see why Miss Case Study here may struggle with taking two. Knowing the best medicine I will ever find is a positive attitude, I try to look at it this way: taking a step backward after taking a step forward is not a disaster; it's simply more of a cha-cha.

I submit my normal Friday blood work at the clinic, and then we head out to Madden's on Gull Lake. Vacationing, we've hit just about every resort in the Brainerd area, but for some reason we hadn't yet been to Madden's. We definitely won't be making that error again. With its beautiful one thousand acres and one mile of shoreline, this property is breathtaking.

It happens that a Willmar High School classmate—Owen Larson—works at Madden's, so I was sure to give him fair warning when we made our reservations. Bob went to check in, and as luck would have it, Owen happened to be behind the desk. Owen followed Bob out to the car, and I had the sheer pleasure of catching up with him for a few minutes. It's quite possible that the last time we saw one another was at our 1985 graduation.

Extending a big hug and catching up on old times, he warmly conveys, "Kelly, I want you to know I'm all caught up on your CaringBridge site, and please know we've been praying for you at church."

I have instant waterworks when I realize this comes from someone I've not seen in thirty-four years.

Our weekend package is for Madden's beautiful honeymoon suite called The Boathouse; it's right on the water. Every night we enjoy watching three loons play right off the end of our dock. The Fairways breakfast buffet is a sight to behold. Oh, and whatever you do, try their crispy country maple bacon and Madden's famous caramel rolls. *You're welcome.* We enjoy their superior staff, explore the grounds, and watch two weddings. Bob gets in a round of golf, and we enjoy a couple's massage. Fact of the matter is that once we check in, we don't want to leave. There's no shame in taking a bit of time out for self-care. With the exception of one night of my not feeling so well, it is an absolute picture-perfect getaway.

Arriving home, I find a familiar box on our front doorstep. Seeing the Precious Moments insignia, I laugh and think of my first trip to the Precious Moments Chapel in Carthage, Missouri, in the early 1990s.

I took a girls' trip with my mom, Aunt Betty Nelson, and Grandma Nelson. Buckled into my green Explorer, we excitedly headed south for a few days. Well, we didn't get too far before the first of many *precious moments* from that road trip occurred. Just south of Albert Lea on I-35, a police helicopter sting was set up, and you guessed it, I got nailed.

Now I'm not sure how many of you have ever been pulled over for speeding with your mom, aunt, and grandma in the car, but I can tell you, it's something you'll never forget. I'm trying hard to keep my composure and talk to the police officer, while the peanut gallery is snickering nonstop. It was a hilarious sight, lifelong memory, and worth every penny of that early 1990s ticket.

When we arrived at the chapel, they encouraged me to sit down and relax on the bench outside. "Oh, the driver must be tired," they persuaded. I no more than sat down when they scampered off into the store. Joke was on me when they returned with a Precious Moments ornament of a police officer writing out a ticket. *Game. Set. Match.*

Back at home now, I open the box to find a large porcelain figurine titled "Caught in the Current of Love." Fittingly, it portrays a couple sharing a special moment in a peaceful outdoor setting, identical to the one Bob and I had enjoyed over the weekend. Precious indeed.

Atta Girl, Alexa

22

June 6–7, 2019

Mighty Mayo again today. Yes, the anxiety leading up to these visits runs high, but good or bad, it's always nice to know where things stand. The more I learn about this disease, the more questions I have. Knowing Dr. Google may not always provide me with the most accurate or in-depth glioblastoma answers, I usually come prepared with a list of questions for Dr. Ruff. But I certainly don't want to waste his precious time. *Hey,* I thought a few days earlier, *what about Alexa?*

Now, I don't completely understand Alexa. Not only that, she scares me. Are we really getting to be that lazy of a society? But I decided to be brave and perform a rapid-fire test before our consult. "Hey, Alexa, why did I burst into tears at the supermarket?" "What's a good name for my tumor?" "Will I squish this thing if I sleep on my right side?" "Is this vertigo I'm experiencing, or should every former blonde not make sudden head movements?" "Do you seriously want me to dance like no one's watching?" "Isn't meditation just a perfect excuse to sit there and do nothing?" "You want to take my temperature *where?*" Whew, not bad. I'm actually getting the hang of this. Who says you can't teach an old dog new tricks?

Cleansing breath in. "Okay, give it to me straight, Alexa. Does the car I used to draw in kindergarten actually exist? Why does the sock I lost in the dryer magically resurface as the lid that fails to fit any plastic container? Customer satisfaction? You want my customer satisfaction? Stop killing trees and asking me to fill out another survey." Exhale. There, I've done it!

"Oh, and Alexa, just one last thing. Why didn't my husband tell me you aren't hooked up yet?" Apparently I've been speaking into a hockey puck this entire time.

In all seriousness, today is another long, information-filled Mayo visit. We rise at 4:30 a.m., and we'll leave the clinic just before 6:00 p.m. Arriving a bit early, we are able to slip in and get my blood work completed ahead of schedule. Good thing, as everything else seems to run a bit behind.

Our first visit is with palliative care. Not being well versed in this area, I am probably on edge. Scratch that, I am *definitely* on edge. Do they know something I don't? Has Dr. Ruff asked them to break some news to me that he can't?

For a couple of weeks my emotions have been running high. The mind can become a dark place if you let it. My first question is, "How is this different from hospice?"

With a sideways smile, Mashele Huschka, a certified nurse practitioner, assures me (a) that this question gets asked all the time and (b) that hospice and palliative care are quite different. Palliative care offers a team-based approach for those learning how to live with a serious or terminal illness. The goal for this group of specialists is simply to help me find my new normal.

In addition to my oncologist and current meds, the palliative care team will address the physical, emotional, social, and spiritual aspects of my new life. Basically, they attempt to alleviate any undue stress. If I have nagging side effects from any current meds or my emotions are running wild, this is my team. It's another level of support or a second set of eyes for my beloved Dr. Ruff, perhaps.

Mashele already has a copy of our health care directives. She comments, "Wow, you've put some time and thought into this."

Funny how inspiring a terminal illness can be.

"Do you have any spiritual questions?" she asks.

No, my Lutheran-loving self answers with a head shake.

"How about your emotions?" she queries.

With a glance at Bob, I admit, "Well, they may not be *perfectly* in check."

Mashele asks, "Do you feel therapy is needed?"

Again, with the shake of my head, I try my best to assure her I'm doing okay and holding my own. *Go easy*, I think, *she has no clue as to this farm girl's lineage.*

"I have to commend you," she says. "You seem as though you're doing quite well."

What she doesn't know is that I've been writing about this journey every step of the way. It's the absolute best therapy in the world, as far as I'm concerned.

Next stop is my eleventh MRI. Those of you who have had MRIs know the cramped conditions. The trouble I experience today is my upper left arm just can't get comfortable. After my three falls at the end of February—one being in the hotel room between a bed and a hard, marble-topped nightstand—my upper left arm still has heightened sensitivity. Lying on my shoulder wrong, pulling on the sleeve of a shirt too quickly, or twisting it a certain way can launch me into outer space.

We try positioning my arm a couple different ways before I'm rolled in for my MRI. Sure enough, I can lie perfectly still for only half of the necessary amount of time. I squeeze the red bulb for the tech to roll me out and ever so carefully readjust my arm. Thankfully, it doesn't affect the results, but talk about feeling like a wimp. Next week's front-burner item is returning to Mayo for an ultrasound to see if I damaged my upper arm. Sigh.

As luck would have it, one of Bob's coworkers and his wife happen to be at Mayo today for a preliminary consult. How nice it is to find a few minutes between appointments and meet them. I remember when we were first-time visitors how overwhelming the facility seemed. But Dave and Karen Johnson seem to feel right at home. Earlier, when inquiring where to find a doughnut and some coffee, they'd received an unsolicited tour from an overly helpful volunteer. Should you ever be at Mayo and have a question, just look for the blue vests.

We arrive at our consult a bit early. While Dr. Ruff is finishing up with another patient, his nurse Rebecca pops her head into our room and introduces herself. Rebecca is someone I've been sending secure portal messages to since October. It is so nice to finally meet! To aid Dr. Ruff's schedule, she comes in to field the questions she can answer.

Sitting on the bench with my crumpled list clenched in my hand, I'm just ready to fire away when Rebecca remarks, "I just love your list of questions; I wish everyone would come in with that!"

As the daughter of two leading list makers, I've always joked that this is a hardwired trait. In a perfect world, I'd probably have a list *for* my lists.

With chemo cycle #5 of seven on the horizon, I'm beginning to see a light at the end of the tunnel. Kinda. I tell Rebecca that I'm worried about the ever-lengthening period of chemo crud. After cycle #4, I had twelve-plus days of downtime. With three cycles left, a girl tends to get a little anxious.

We talk about going on heavier nausea meds and perhaps adding a muscle relaxer. Not that I have a ton of muscle mass left to relax, but for some reason my neck and upper shoulders remain bothersome.

We also discuss my tanking platelets. Today mine are at 47, but they should be in the 100 to 400 range. Chemo's catch-22 is that your platelets need to be high enough to undergo chemo so the chemo can treat your disease. But chemo destroys your platelets. It's an ever-revolving door.

Dr. Ruff knocks, apologizes for the wait, and dives right in—an approach I've appreciated about him all along: "Well, Kelly, your scan today isn't quite as good as when I saw you two months ago, but it's better than your first one postsurgery."

Pulling up my scans, he highlights that the remnants of the tumor have not grown, and he's happy to see there are no new areas popping up. But he does see a darker gray area behind the tumor area—possible swelling that wasn't visible on the image during our April visit.

Dr. Ruff encourages me to (a) go back on 2 mg of the steroid dexamethasone immediately to help with swelling, (b) go back to twice-weekly blood draws in Chaska until my platelets improve, and (c) give my body a break from the harsh regimen of receiving a dual dose of chemo. He is happy to hear I haven't experienced any more balance issues due to what he believes is swelling.

Knowing Dr. Ruff wouldn't administer chemo unless my platelets are above 100, I had been sensing a time-out might be in order.

Shoot, I probably won't be done with chemo by my September 3 birthday, I reflect. It was a small goal, but still a goal. This feeling crummy for close to a year tends to cramp a girl's style.

I feel slightly guilt ridden, as though I haven't completed all my homework since our last visit. But Dr. Ruff assures me there isn't a lot I can do to raise my platelet levels.

Dr. Ruff then asks if there is any paperwork he can help with. "I want to keep you as stress-free as possible," he explains.

I shake my head. "No, my SSDI unbelievably was approved in four days, and the investigation for some additional insurance coverage should be wrapping up shortly."

"Great," the good doctor responds. "Then can I see you back here in a month? I'd like to keep a little closer eye on things."

As you wish, Dr. Ruff, as you wish.

With my next chemo cycle in flux, I sense there's an ebb and a flow to these glioblastoma treatments. It unfortunately prevents me from accepting invites to the many nice lunches and get-togethers offered. This lengthy process is better taken in a series of baby steps than in a race where the quickest sprinter wins. We can't rush or control a thing. Ah, except attitude. Attitude we can control.

How fortunate I am that Bob continues to take absolutely *everything* in stride. The small celebrations, the temporary pitfalls, my wreaking havoc on his work schedule, and this messy person I am slowly beginning to recognize as me.

On our drive home, I text family with my less-than-fist-pumping results for the day. In bright brotherly fashion, Ryan reminds me: "One day at a time. The only prescriptions you need to keep filled are FAITH and HOPE."

Copy that, little bro, copy that.

Putting the Pieces Together

23

June 13, 2019

Pieces are slowly falling into place. It's been a haul up until this point, and with God's grace, it just might be a haul that continues a while longer. No one ever knows, and I'm certainly no exception.

Yesterday's ultrasound at Mayo showed no blood clots in my upper arm, which Bob and I quickly add to the win column. Once my platelet levels recover—granted, they have a ways to go before I can begin my next chemo cycle—I have the go-ahead to begin physical therapy for my left hand's fine-motor skills and my upper arm.

Another thing that is nice to finally wrap up is the supplemental insurance determination. After months of calls, mounds of paperwork, file transfers, and UPS mailings, it will be nice to step back into my *real job* of fighting this cancerous brain tumor. I understand why the intensive form-filling needs to be done, but the added stress gets to be a lot. I empathize with every fighter out there who experiences this overwhelming feeling.

If given the chance, how would I advise others traveling this surreal GBM4 journey?

- Remind yourself that it's not your fault. You were hit with the deadliest form of brain cancer, not seasonal allergies.
- Yes, the well-intentioned messages "Let me know what I can do" and "Keep me posted" will sound somewhat

empty when you're fighting to get out of bed.
Encourage friends just to check in themselves.

- Protect your caregiver from burnout. Don't be afraid to ask others for help. The longer you fight, the further people drift. Life does go on, after all.
- Be gentle with yourself—set boundaries if necessary.
- Recognize the importance of health insurance and having no lapse in plans.
- Save for a rainy day. Most households don't anticipate one major medical occurrence, let alone two.
- Make a conscious decision to rejoice and celebrate life— every day!

My final bit of good news for today comes in an email update from the National Brain Tumor Society. The US Senate took quick action and approved the resolution to designate July 17, 2019, as Glioblastoma Awareness Day in America. We are making a name, we are getting a face, and national leaders are understanding the urgency for action to find a cure for this terrible disease that impacts thousands.

Platelet Mambo:
How Low Can You Go?

June 21, 2019

Evidently these platelets have a mind of their own and insist on becoming an issue. Since my last Mayo consult, my morning routine has been the same: visit Minnesota Oncology in Chaska; check in with Patty; have a spirited conversation with my lab tech, Deb; demonstrate the Platelet Prance on my way back to the waiting room (inventing a goofy dance can only help, right?); sit patiently in my lucky chair; and then see if the sheet comes back stamped with the words *Critical Result* in red.

This week I am consistent, albeit consistently low. Platelet draws are 25, 28, 20, 23, and 32. Not my best work, but at least the number is higher heading into the weekend.

Earlier in the week, Mayo nurse Katrina and I discussed the necessary logistics for having a blood transfusion, if deemed necessary. Upon learning that Minnesota Oncology does not perform the blood type match at their facility, I suggested heading back to the scene of the crime where this whole mess started—Park Nicollet Methodist Hospital and Frauenshuh Cancer Center. Turns out, the more clinics and hospitals we get involved, the more complicated the process is becoming for Mayo with ordering, authorizing, and managing red tape in general. I assured Katrina I certainly didn't mind driving to Rochester for a transfusion on a beautiful summer day.

It's abundantly clear Dr. Ruff wants these pesky platelets to rebound on their own. While I'm not exactly *eager* to begin chemo cycle #5, it would keep the ball rolling. Dr. Ruff optimistically believes I am rounding the platelet bend, and he gives me the same weekend assignment: should I see the slightest sign of blood—from my gums after brushing, from blowing my nose, from unexplained bruising, or in stools—I am to go directly to the emergency room. "Oh, and Deb should see you back on Monday for another draw." With my minimum platelet count goal of 100 to reinstate chemo cycles, I'll be doing some serious power praying over the weekend.

Unbelievably, the bright side to this platelet mambo is that I feel *really* good taking a break. Four or five weeks past chemo cycle #4, I see signs of feeling human again. It gives me hope as to how I might feel once more of these drugs filter out of my body. I have been able to plan a few last-minute iced tea encounters and lovely impromptu lunches with friends who previously had taken a back seat. May you forever know just how much I appreciate your gift of light and love.

Emotional Mess Express

25

June 22, 2019

On this emotional journey, I've been fortunate to keep most things in perspective—until today, that is.

First I am asked a rather out-of-the-blue, brain-stumping question: "Do you think you'll ever be able to return to work part-time?" Now, if I had the necessary insight to answer that question, it certainly would make dealing with this whole cancer fiasco a lot easier. "I'm only one month into SSDI, and I'm not sure of any reputable places to buy a crystal ball, so I have no idea," I attempt to explain with humor. But seriously, the thing with glioblastomas, to say nothing of grade 4 tumors, is that you don't know if you have five days, five months, or five years. Truth be told, *none* of us have that kind of insight, but questions like this set off my touchy, ticking emotional time bomb.

It just so happens this question lands the same day I'm coordinating the return of my work items. Unbeknownst to the good-intentioned inquirer, it's bad timing.

Next comes a wonderful time with dear friends where the conversation turns toward Thanksgiving plans and winter 2020 vacations. Already? A brief bit of envy surfaces in me. After all, for the majority of my life, the planner extraordinaire has been me! But fresh from a week-plus of plummeting platelets clouding my everyday outlook, I sadly can't handle this conversation tonight. I've never been an overly sensitive person, nor do I ever *want* to be. But friends, if I could kindly ask one thing, maybe take a moment and consider your audience.

With tough feelings like these, I'm grateful we made it to Lord of Life Church tonight. Each time we attend, we walk away knowing exactly why we're supposed to be there, and tonight is no exception.

We find ourselves in the first occupied row of our church pew section—foreign territory to us Lutherans. During the offertory, Amy Cerepak from the praise band steps up to the microphone, and with the voice of an angel, she beautifully sings "Someone's Praying Me Through." By the second stanza, I am a bawling mess. A shoulder-shaking, silent-sobbing, nose-running mess.

With nowhere to hide and unfortunately no tissue in sight, I try to wipe away my steady stream of uncontrollable tears. Each and every emotion, diagnosis, and test result since October 13, 2018, speedily passes through my brain like a movie trailer during that four-minute song. My reaction is so raw and yet so releasing.

Amy and I lock eyes at one point. She probably wonders what on earth my problem is. While our eyes don't—or can't—meet again, somewhere during her gift of music the words change from "someone's praying *me* through" to "someone's praying *you* through." Whether she did that intentionally or not, I will be letting her know what a blessing her gift of song is to me. She touches my heart in a way that none other could tonight.

I grasp my husband's hand tighter; we know it is the perfect song for my not-so-perfect day.

We Are Stronger Together

26

June 26, 2019

This next bit of information I'm sharing is not intended as a request for more help for Bob and me. But hopefully this advice will help you support a family member, friend, or complete stranger traveling down a similar path.

Fortunately, in both of our cases—POEMS in 2012 and now GBM4 beginning in 2018—we found ourselves abundantly blessed with assistance from others. One doesn't need to invest much time on a support group site to realize that's far from typical.

Many family, friends, and colleagues want to know how they can help during a time of desperate need. They ask; we shrug. It's a combination of not knowing what's needed and perhaps not knowing how it will be received. Everyone wants to help, but few know what to do.

Here are some suggestions from the other side of the fence. Know beyond a shadow of a doubt, any fighter and their over-extended caregiver would be eternally grateful to receive any one of these.

Bare basics grocery shopping. Think paper towels, laundry detergent, bread, juice, eggs, bananas. . . . Shop in store or order online and have it delivered to their home. Forget about brands, specific tastes, or questioning whether something is what your loved one would like or not. Indecisiveness like that prevents your follow-through. When some caregivers can't be gone long enough to run out and purchase toilet paper or milk to settle a queasy patient's stomach, they will kiss you for bringing it to their door. Trust me.

After Bob's stem cell transplant in 2012, we were returning home from six weeks in our Rochester rental. I'll never forget Bev and Dan Faulkner calling and asking us for our garage code. They took it upon themselves to stock our refrigerator and pantry with a few staples. What an unbelievable blessing when we were running ragged.

Offering rides to treatments. We were lucky with logistics, as well as to have an unbelievably understanding employer for my caregiving husband—my never-ending thanks to the owners of Richlind Metal Fabricators. Again, it's not the norm. Many caregivers juggle full-time jobs and may have added hurdles, such as busy meeting or travel schedules. Receiving the gift of transportation on a hectic day brings a huge sigh of relief.

Babysitting or offering to take school-aged children for a few hours. So here is where I'm speaking to something I know nothing about. I can only imagine what this road is like for a mother or father who needs help with young children. Taking the kids for an impromptu sleepover or Saturday morning outing may give your struggling loved ones the rest and quiet they need.

Bringing a meal or working with a group of friends to organize meals. Basic dishes that are easy to freeze and reheat become lifesavers. Toss-away aluminum pans or reusable plastic containers that don't need returning are a plus. Since visitors can be tiresome and germs are a factor, offer to leave meals in a cooler outside their door.

Pet-sitting or plant watering. Again, here's something I know nothing about, but I've heard pet boarding is expensive. If you know your loved one is going out of town for a procedure or appointment, offer to care for their furry family members. Should you be one of the green thumbs of the world wishing to help, volunteer to water interior or exterior plants.

Texting an inspiring quote. We warriors need all the encouragement we can get, and hearing from you means the world to us. A few kind words—especially a question-free message not requiring a return response—breaks up our day and lets us know we are loved.

Considering the caregivers. Their lives have dramatically changed too. Invite them to a game, a car show, a round of golf, a cup of coffee, or a simple Sunday afternoon drive, just as you did before. Just because their spouse isn't up for getting out of the house doesn't mean they aren't or can't. The break will mean a lot to them. If it's not a good time for a break, they'll let you know. They will appreciate the gesture, as well as the glimpse of normalcy.

Mailing a gift card. Unexpected expenses—extra gas for treatment travel, extra meals out, astronomical medical bills—take a huge toll on every patient's budget. Any gas, grocery, gift, restaurant, hardware store, or hobby/craft store gift card is a welcome surprise. If your loved ones enjoy reading or music, Amazon or iTunes cards could provide new entertainment to get them through long treatment sessions. A prepaid Visa gift card is perfect for helping out with medical copays.

Paying for a onetime service or volunteering a few hours of your time cleaning, mowing lawn, removing snow, washing windows, doing holiday decorating, etc. This is the perfect service opportunity for helpful teenage kids. If the kids have trusted supervision, the job could be done while the family is away at treatment or out of town.

If you have a willing employer, donating some vacation time. Unpaid leave is sure to cause additional financial hardship. If donating a vacation day or two is an option, drum up a few employees to see if they might be willing to do the same. It is sure to help the patient or caregiver navigating major medical, mortgage, and household expenses.

Thinking soft and cuddly. If knitting is your thing, consider making a prayer shawl, soft cap, or socks. Thoughtful gifts like a new set of slippers, pajamas, pull-on pants, or V neck T-shirts (allowing easier port access) would be a definite plus. Pamper your loved ones with items that are cozy and comfortable.

Sending snail mail. Nothing brightens a day more than finding a hand-addressed note in the mail among the medical bills. Recognizing the handwriting and return address will instantly bring joy to your loved ones' hearts.

Donating blood in their name. Cancer and other illnesses prohibit patients from donating, so we appreciate the throngs of you who do donate that much more.

Hosting a scarf and hat party. This suggestion comes from my online support groups. Maybe it's a regional trend, but I'm pretty sure it would be viewed as a welcome celebration for anyone worried about losing hair. Bring together close friends, light refreshments, and a variety of headwear options. What's not to love? It's sure to make the transition easier. Kindly take into consideration treatment cycles and when your guest of honor might be feeling best.

While this list is a bit more extensive than I intended, my hope is to inspire the countless people who claim they just don't know what to do. Throughout life, especially in times of hardship, we are definitely stronger together than we are apart. Personally, I simply appreciate every thoughtful person who takes the time to act.

The Here and Now

Present Day

I am grateful to be able to say that this story remains unfinished. It absolutely is true that what doesn't kill you makes you stronger. Through these circumstances, I've learned that I'm a fighter, and I believe in mind over matter. I see obstacles as hurdles in life that are meant to be jumped over, not to stop us. I serve an amazing and ever-watchful God, am so fortunate to have a remarkable husband, and am loved beyond measure by my family and many, many treasured friends.

Never will you catch me being ashamed of my scar. It's a vivid reminder that this farm girl is far stronger than what tried to destroy me. I find I am braver because I stood toe to toe with the giant, stronger because I simply had to be, and happier because I've learned what, to say nothing of *who*, truly matters.

I've worked hard to avoid thinking, *Why me?* Why not me? Each and every one of us has battles. My current state is no worse and no more important than yours; it's just different. I've come to grips with the fact that the boxes next to Brain Tumor and Cancer will forever be checked on future medical questionnaires. I've also learned it's okay if life isn't exactly what you thought it might be.

Recently someone reminded me that the name Kelly means "brave warrior." Fitting, perhaps? Certainly not on the days when I have to sweet-talk myself into getting out of bed or when I feel entitled to at least a participation ribbon just for walking to the mailbox. I do have my moments.

Occasionally I've heard the comment, "I don't know how you do it." Plain and simple, I wasn't given a choice. Absolutely no one knows how strong they are until being strong is the only choice they have. The pact I've made with myself is that I'm not giving up and I'm not giving in. Scandinavians can be stubborn that way.

One thing I confess: the longer I've been able to absorb the idea that this disease is never going away, the more I realize my filters are changing. Just a bit. The logical side of my brain cautions, *Um, don't say it, don't say it, don't say it,* while my injured side prods, *Oh, what the heck; let's just see what happens here.*

I did reach a point where I was tired of living in fear. If we're keeping things in perspective, fear itself can kill too. Occasionally I'll remind myself that the tumor isn't the result of some personal failing; it's simply the luck of the draw, no different than Bob's diagnosis was. Even on off days I prefer to keep putting on the boxing gloves and stepping into the ring. With this disease dictating so many things, it's important to teach oneself how to live *with* an illness, not *in spite of* an illness. While I have absolutely no idea how long I have, I am determined to be a resourceful GBM4 patient for as long as I am given. My goal is to let people know, teach them how to care, and share the experience of this unchartered journey.

I have grandiose goals of eventually getting back to exercising. Some days my teeter-totter votes sit more on the side of adding muscle strength; other days I find them at the opposite end, longing for low-impact cardio activities I could do with ease prediagnosis. On busy workdays I was tracking sixteen thousand steps a day. Not only do I miss that at-least-you've-done-something-good-for-today feeling, but I hate that activity has come to a screeching halt.

When my dad passed sixteen years ago, it took months before I was in the right frame of mind to get back on the exercise wagon. He would always call me bright and early on weekdays before he stepped outside, knowing he'd be in a John Deere tractor cab all day. Almost always I was on the treadmill before work when he called. For months I associated exercising with the loss of my father. It took time. Now, unsure how my brain balance will react to a treadmill or elliptical machine, I continue to take things slowly. I pray I will eventually find my way back with the self-assurance of a little girl wearing a Wonder Woman T-shirt.

Since I am no longer able to tie a shoe, my first order of business will be to find some Velcro sneakers, just like my nephew Harris's. Definite sneaker envy set in when I laid my eyes on those little gems. I've misplaced forty to forty-five pounds, depending on the week, and now kick myself for making a trip into Goodwill with a bag of my smaller jeans just prior to Diagnosis Day.

I still enjoy getting up early with Bob on weekdays. That's not to say I don't snooze for a while after he leaves, but I like to make him a cup of coffee, pack his lunch, fix him a travel glass of ice water, and make sure the house alarm is off before a sleepy someone heads out the door. Not one day goes by that he doesn't say, "Sweetie, thanks for doing my stuff." It's that simple space in time when the ordinary suddenly seems extraordinary.

I've learned I certainly don't envy doctors. Delivering bad news can't be any easier than receiving bad news. "Eh, it's just brain surgery," said no one ever. I'm guessing it has to be a refined skill of sorts, but one they probably never get used to.

It's pretty safe to say that all cancer, regardless of ribbon color, stinks. The first day of our journey, we decide whether we prefer to be victims or survivors. Mustering up all the strength we have, we set out to fight this fight we know nothing about and make a conscious choice to remain positive and not let cancer define us.

You've read enough by now to know the statistical data is not stellar by any means. I can only hope I'm one of those amazing glioblastoma survival stories and am a person who is given a chance to go on and live their best second-chance life.

Until then I have chosen to document ways that may help Bob navigate life without me: how to boil water, where I keep an updated list of passwords, how to set up and use bill pay, where to view direct deposits, where to find our monthly expense spreadsheet if he chooses to continue it, how to place an order with our best friend Amazon Prime, where the extra rolls of toilet paper are stashed, and how to record a program on a DVR. You know, important stuff. A somewhat gloomy approach perhaps, but this is a grace period I honestly feel privileged to have.

Lucky for me, Bob has never been one to keep score, or my similar list would be much longer: how to start up the sprinklers, how to turn on the fire pit, when to replace the furnace filter, how to sync cell phones in cars, what chemicals are necessary for hot tub maintenance, how to reset our internet connection, where the DIRECTV box is located, how to replace the ink cartridges in our printer, how to set the landscape light timer, how to "summerize" the snow blower, how to put air in the tires, how to obtain access to the safe, how to set the automatic thermostat, and most important, how to enlist a little thing called patience and talk nice to snarky customer service people over the phone.

Given the option, would I prefer to be privy to my ETA at heaven's door? I'm completely on the fence about that one. There are a couple different ways to approach such insider information. Either you can feel like a ticking time bomb, or you can model yourself after a well-known Tim McGraw song: go skydiving, climb mountains, renew relationships, and simply spend more time doing the things you love. Neither approach is wrong, just different. Whatever the approach, you do you.

The thing I do know is that I've given my prayer warriors job security. I picture one day meeting our Lord and Savior at heaven's gate and hearing His greeting: "Farm girl, you've kept Me busy." Allow yourself to burn the new candles, drag out the good dishes, and wear your favorite perfume—just don't kill any canaries. I have quickly learned it's completely okay to let go of the life you thought you'd live and find sheer joy in the story you have.

Just as a musician remarks about the song they wrote overnight, these words were written within a few weeks. Had I had two cooperating typing hands, I would have shaved off some serious time. Putting thoughts down on paper is incredibly therapeutic. I've asked Bob to read a paragraph here or there to see if what I was trying to say came across correctly. "I so respect you for being able to do this, Kelly. I don't know that I could," he'd reply. While writing this down may not be the easiest route, it has become a wonderfully self-reflective one.

I am thrilled to see that some things will never change. Thankfully, my brothers and nephews continue to view me as an easy target at family functions and have yet to let up on poking fun at me. So what if I recently spent twenty minutes searching for my phone in the car while using the flashlight on my phone? That's beside the point.

My dad always used to say, "The second we stop picking on you, you'll know there's something wrong." Much like the sun rising in the east and setting in the west, it's something I appreciate about this lovable, huggable bunch. While I may not have the blonde hair anymore, I do have a valid brain tumor card. And I'm not afraid to use it!

As you may have guessed, I would have hated to lose my sense of humor through all this. I choose to embrace pain with kindness, respond to things wicked with whimsy. Bottom out my platelet levels or make me lose function of my left hand/arm, okay, but do not mess with my humor.

Little did we all know, adulting is really hard work some days. Life is certainly not what I imagined as a blue-eyed, pig-tailed, freckle-faced little kid. Thankfully, my faith, humor, and optimism have allowed me to KOKO (keep on keeping on). Now, that's an acronym this farm girl can get used to.

I survived a cancerous brain tumor. So what's your super-power?

Epilogue

My cancerous brain tumor journey is far from a solo one and pales in comparison to the roller coaster that some have been on. When I made the decision to dig a little deeper on this project, it wasn't with the intent of closing a chapter, but opening up a heart. This hopeful, broken, prayerful, beating, exposed, appreciative, OCD, nervous, hurting, optimistic, anxious, angry, guarded, faith-driven heart.

When things began coming together and I could foresee a finished project possibly on the horizon, I knew this sometimes blonde was in way over her head. Lucky for me, I know people. My friend Lois Wallentine has worked in publishing for thirty years. Being ninety-five days apart in age and growing up together in Mamrelund Lutheran Church, we've known each other since we were toddlers.

I'm told the first time we sang together in church was around the age of four, and not long after that, our mothers began dressing us alike. Joke was on them, however, when well into our upper teens we'd inadvertently purchase similar if not the exact same clothing as the other. And no, we weren't scheduled to sing together anytime soon. Lois had only brothers, and I had only brothers, so our easy, breezy childhood days consisted of securing playhouse privacy, eating grilled cheese sandwiches and chocolate pudding, scoring perfect attendance at each other's birthday parties, riding horses and three-wheelers, and having sleepovers. Many, many sleepovers. Our farm families are

friends, so we also attended the same 4-H functions and, after I moved, Willmar High School. It took me a while to connect the dots, but who better to edit this hot mess of a memoir than someone who has known me my entire life?

To Lois, my forever friend, from the bottom of my childhood heart, I thank you for your meaningful insight, thought-provoking suggestions, expertise in the field, willingness to help a homie, and passionate perception to convey what has become my real life.

To Diane Hart, I am humbly in awe. Having not even met, we happen to share a mutual friend named Lois. When approached, you instantly agreed to design this book cover and relayed that you'd be honored to work on such a personal piece. Coincidentally enough, you've worked at Mayo Clinic for twenty-four years, currently as senior manager in Media Support Services. I'm so happy to make this new *Hart*-felt connection, and I'm so grateful to you for sharing your time and talents.

To all the caregiving spouses, partners, and parents living with cancer patients, you are the unsung heroes. While I may have experience on both sides of the coin (caregiver and caregivee), I can assure you that not even your closest of friends know what you are truly going through. Life suddenly has land mines. That's the unforgiving side of disease.

To my family, I feel so bad for putting you through any of this. I appreciate all your time, miles, visits, tears, suggestions, research, and evident unconditional love. Knowing full well that I wasn't, you made me feel as though I was the only person on your radar during my time of need. Rarely does cancer have a face until it affects someone you know. I am forever fortunate to be loved by you all and to claim you as family.

And to Bob, my happily ever after, my safe place to fall. You have been my rock, my calm in the storm, and an unwavering pillar of strength. Somehow you know just what to say and just what to do. I don't know how you manage to keep your composure as some of these scenarios occur, but you do so with extreme grace. Thank you for holding me as I wept, encouraging me when I was down, and empathetically understanding why *our* life has changed. I seriously didn't know that a heart could open up much more.

Always the Mr. Fixit, you've had the tougher job of watching me fight a battle you can do nothing about. Broken-bodied or not, neither POEMS nor a cancerous glioblastoma brain tumor can break us. I realize you didn't sign up for this, nor did we ever see ourselves in this scenario, but boy, do you shine. Every time you sit shaking your head and tell me, "It hurts my heart to see you going through this," I know deep down just how genuine your words are. You've been there. You, my love, are the one who's above average. I thank you every day for continuing to love me for the farm girl that I am.

If the best view comes from the hardest climb,
what a sight to behold it will be.

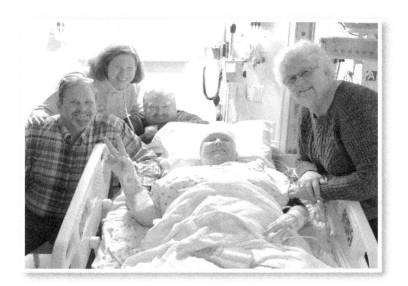

My sincere thanks, dear reader,
for traveling this road beside me.

A share of the proceeds from this book
will benefit brain tumor research.